# Leadership

# in Residential Child Care

BY THE SAME AUTHOR

*Working in Group Care.*
*Social Work in Residential and Day Care Settings*

*What Works in Residential Child Care*
(with Roger Bullock and Roger Clough)

*Therapeutic Communities for Children and Young People*
(edited with Alan Worthington, Jane Pooley
and Kajetan Kasinski)

*Helping People in Family Centres: Towards Therapeutic Practice*
(edited with Linnet McMahon)

*Intuition is not Enough:*
*Matching Learning with Practice in Therapeutic Child Care*
(edited with Linnet McMahon)

*Relationship-based Social Work: Getting to the Heart of Practice*
(edited with Gillian Ruch and Danielle Turney)

# Leadership in Residential Child Care

## A relationship-based approach

ADRIAN WARD

Smokehouse Press, Norwich

Published by Smokehouse Press, Norwich, 2014
www.smokehousepress.co.uk

Typeset in Lucida Bright and Gill Sans

Printed and bound in the UK by
Berforts Information Press Ltd



ISBN 9780957633537

# Contents

# Introduction

> A young person storms off to her room, shouting obscenities about her mother ... an essential staff meeting is repeatedly disrupted by a series of domestic and staffing crises ... a group of children go on the rampage, leaving the staff team and their manager in a state of despair and despondency ...

It is at moments like these that leadership is called for - to help staff work out what to do next, to support them through the crisis, and to keep everyone's eye on the overall task. This book is about how leaders can do all of this while also staying sane, focused and resourceful themselves.

Working in children's homes, and other residential care settings, is tough, emotional and fraught with risks, and being the leader of the team providing such care is especially difficult. In the familiar phrase, 'the buck stops here': the leader is responsible - and will be held accountable - for everything that happens in the place. He or she will need to be quick-witted, insightful and resilient, and will have to provide both support and control on a day-to-day-basis as well as steering the ship through frequent dramatic incidents, all the time keeping in mind the overall aim of the work: providing care, support and treatment for young people in the midst of enormous difficulty in their lives and helping them on their way to a better future.

So in this short book I will be exploring what is involved in this challenging leadership role, offering what will at times be a very personal account, drawing not only on my own experience, but also on many other examples from practice such as the ones outlined above. I will be taking a relationship-based approach - in other words, one which emphasizes the quality of the human interactions between the leader and the others involved, at both an emotional and a practical level. My aim is to identify some of the challenges and difficulties that may arise, and to examine what people on all sides often seem to be seeking from their leader, as well as how the leader can manage and respond to these expectations.

The book is intended primarily for those employed in senior roles in residential child care services, whether at unit manager, deputy or team leader level, but also for those with external responsibilities for the support, oversight and inspection of these services. The provision of residential child care, both in the UK and elsewhere, has dwindled significantly over the last thirty years with the growth of fostering and adoption. However, there still remains, and will probably always remain, a small number of children for whom residential care may be the best and (for some of the children themselves) the preferred option.

The book focuses very largely on the specific context of residential care, since this is the area of my most substantial experience, and since this is a context that brings such distinctive challenges. At the same time I would argue that much of what is contained here will also be applicable in many other settings, and especially in the wide range of services in which children and young people are placed in the care and protection of others, such as family centres, boarding schools and other educational, psychiatric and health care centres. Later in this chapter I will outline the nature of the specific task in residential child care, but readers from non-childcare settings will hopefully also find many parallels in relation to - for example - other residential services including those for older people or for people with learning difficulties, and possibly in other professional settings, too. I have discussed some of these parallels more fully in my book *Working in Group Care* (2006).

I should explain that this is not primarily an academic text but a practical one, aimed at helping leaders and those supporting them to think more deeply about their work. So I am not seeking to offer a comprehensive review of the literature on leadership, or to focus much on comparing or analysing 'models' or theories of leadership. In fact there is not much literature that does focus directly on leadership in the residential context. Instead, I will be looking closely at the main issues as they arise in practice, and drawing upon anonymised examples from the workplace, to show how some key concepts may be helpful in making sense of the whole experience. I will also focus on the personal and professional demands and expectations often experienced in the job. Indeed we will start - in Chapter 1 - where all leaders start: with the experience of becoming a leader and discovering what the role means for oneself as well as for the others involved.

To understand the approach adopted in this book, let us for the moment imagine the subject of leadership as an area of land, using the metaphor of the 'territory' in which leaders have to operate. My concern in this book is firstly to *map out* this territory, discovering how extensive it is and how varied and unpredictable it can be. Secondly I want to explore what seems to be going on *within* the territory - the relationships, the power issues and the ways in which, for instance, certain patterns and roles may emerge, in other words 'how the land lies'. Thirdly I also want to go '*below* the surface' of the territory to look at some of the less obvious ways in which leaders are perceived both by themselves and by others, and at how these unconscious dynamics may affect the success or otherwise of the whole enterprise. It is not my intention to come up with a route map of the whole terrain. and in any case I don't believe that could be done, since every leader's experience will be different. Still less will I try to provide a full checklist of what you may need to take with you on the journey, but rather to report back from my own journey and reflections with some traveller's tales and other thoughts about what might be learned from the experiences described.

**Leadership and management**

It also seems important at the outset to make some distinction between management and leadership. The problem is, of course, that in practice there is often considerable overlap between these topics, because managers always have to exert some degree of leadership, although the converse is not quite true: not all of those who may provide leadership are actually employed as managers. For example, at ground level in residential child care, staff often have to take on temporary leadership roles in the heat of the moment as a situation develops. At times like this, someone needs to take control and help others – both staff and young people – to work together at resolving their difficulties. But having done this, these temporary leaders are then likely to revert to their more familiar role, rather than thereby becoming managers.

It is also true that there may be intermediate leadership roles within staff teams, with team leaders, assistant managers and others all holding some responsibility for leadership in certain areas. So while most of what I will be discussing in this book will concentrate on the leadership aspects of the formal position of manager or 'head of home', much of it can also be applied to these other levels and types of leadership.

The distinction commonly made between management and leadership is that whereas management is about planning, organising and overseeing, leadership is about developing the vision that will inform all that planning, the sense of strategy to ensure that it actually works, and the personal qualities of engagement, inspiration and attention to team issues such as morale that are so critical in getting the work done. The best text on residential management is John Burton's *Handbook of Managing Residential Care* (1997), and a useful research-based book is by Leslie Hicks et al, *Managing Children's Homes* (2007); both of these books do also touch on questions of leadership. (NB See also Richard Rollinson's account (2003) of his experience in leadership, and a much earlier slim volume by Jones [1970]).

So perhaps we can now adapt the 'terrain' metaphor somewhat, to think of the team setting off on a journey: if a group of people of varying levels of experience, seniority and skill were heading off on a challenging hill-walk together, they would probably benefit enormously from the leadership of an experienced guide. This sort of guide or leader will not always be walking at the front or calling out orders, but may be just as effective at times by walking alongside people, demonstrating confidence in the route and enthusiasm for the enterprise, as well as by showing an understanding of any risks and challenges that may arise. Indeed, such a leader might well encourage others in the party to try out and develop their own leadership potential at times, and might take opportunities as these arise to support and informally educate people in this aspect of their development. At the same time, this leader might also play the more specific role of a 'manager' in the sense of (for example) securing and deploying the resources needed to see the group through the whole trip, although of course mere management would not be enough once they were up on the hillside with the mists closing in.

To push the 'terrain' metaphor one step further, people would probably place most value on a leader who knew the ground well, who was familiar with the sorts of situations that might arise and resourceful in terms of ways of handling any eventuality - but they would also want someone who could remain human and concerned for them as people rather than solely for him/herself or for the formal aims of the project. In other words, someone who really understands people and is able to communicate with them effectively even when things are not going well.

This last point highlights one aspect of the tensions that a leader has to negotiate, between *leading the group of people* and *leading the task* which they are employed to achieve - this distinction is sometimes formulated as the 'expressive' versus the 'instrumental' aspects of leadership respectively. In the real world, of course, successful leadership brings these elements together and promotes confidence in the whole team so that they can rightly say 'we did it ourselves' (Lao Tsu, 1972).

**Inside and outside**

We will be looking at the sorts of expectations that the team and the leader may have of each other at various levels, as well as at other types of leadership role including the vital relationships with external bodies such as the employing and regulatory organisations, and with other professionals as well as with the young people's families and the neighbourhood. The fact that leaders constantly have to straddle the boundary between the 'inside' and the 'outside' of the unit is just one example of the many ways in which they have to divide their attentions between different groupings and different levels of thinking and operating. One hazard of constantly moving between different groups and tasks is that you may never spend enough time in any one of them to become fully identified with it, with the risk that you may become isolated and thus less effective as a leader. Again, successful leaders will avoid such hazards by integrating the inner and the outer focus.

### The nature of the residential task

Because this book concentrates on this specific area of practice rather than being a generic discussion of leadership, I also want to make some introductory remarks about the nature of the residential task with children.

A children's home could be described as a small and intense human organisation, providing care, warmth and support for separated children, and focused on addressing the emotional pain and the other challenges which they face as well as supporting them towards some resolution of whatever crisis they have been in, and enabling them to move on to the next stage in their lives. We cannot think usefully about the leadership of these places without remaining firmly aware of the nature of their task. A children's home is plainly not a bureaucratic or industrial undertaking, engaged in the processing of data or physical materials, nor is it primarily an educational or leisure-oriented organisation providing emotionally 'neutral' learning or recreational experience. Its clientele are by definition those young people in our society who have experienced -and in many cases still are experiencing - some of the very greatest disruption and distress. Although we must not overlook the fact that they are also 'just children' who need plenty of opportunities to enjoy the ordinary pleasures and achievements of everyday life, the challenging reality is that these particular children bring with them all of the distress arising from their disrupted lives, bringing these feelings not only into the very fabric of the building but also into the whole system of human interaction in the place.

I am emphasizing this aspect of the emotional task because it has enormous significance for the nature and pace of the work which the child care team has to undertake with the young people twenty-four hours a day, and therefore it also has important implications for the kind of support and leadership that the team will need.

It is for this reason that when thinking about leadership in this context we must draw on ideas from well beyond the standard 'business leadership' literature, in which the raw materials are usually inert or neutral and with little or no emotional significance for the staff. A child care team, by contrast, may have to soak up or respond to some extreme emotions in the course of any given day's work; and often with very little notice, and because they themselves are human they may be personally and quite deeply affected by some of this distress and disturbance, sometimes without fully realising it at the time. This everyday reality means that the child care staff will need the support and encouragement of very skilled leadership if they are to be enabled not just to withstand the stress but also to remain responsive and positive in their work.

The corollary of this situation is that the leadership role can be one with a high level of demand and potentially a degree of isolation. Leaders often find themselves on the boundary between the inside and the outside, or mediating between different groups and groupings, and indeed to some extent this is where they need to position themselves. The patron saint of leaders would probably be Janus, the Roman god of doorways, who had two faces, one looking in and the other looking outwards, which may sound quite uncomfortable but probably sounds familiar to anyone who has held a leadership role. Leaders may also sometimes have to hold confidential information about change, for instance, and they often find themselves in the middle of everybody's strong feelings, both conscious and unconscious.

For this reason what is most important is that leaders themselves have regular and reliable access to supervision and consultation, and throughout this book I will be emphasizing both of these equally. It is the proper responsibility of external line managers to ensure that residential leaders have regular supervision on all aspects of their work, including the opportunity to reflect on its psychological and emotional demands. Unfortunately many residential leaders still do not have access to this sort of supervision.

Secondly, and I think even more rare in practice, I have always argued that residential leaders should also have access to independent consultation on their role and task, again including the emotional component. The point here is that the demands of the job require leaders to be able to stand right back from the whole system at times, and to review and evaluate their own experience and contribution. Supervision within the organisation is important, but equally so is external consultation.

## The context of care

Alongside these enduring truths about the emotional task of care, we also need to keep in mind the always-changing context within which this care is provided. The profile of residential child care has changed enormously in the last thirty years, across most western countries and especially in the UK, which will be my main focus in this book. For several reasons the number of young people in children's homes has dropped dramatically over this period, and those in care now are more likely to be older, more troubled and from a more diverse background than they might have been in the past. The sector is also much more highly regulated and closely inspected than in previous times, and while these changes may have addressed anxieties about the risks of poor or abusive practice, they may also have inhibited creative and holistic practice in some respects. Indeed much of what has been written in recent years about residential care has necessarily concentrated very largely on 'safety' and child protection issues, but sometimes to the extent that both leaders and residential staff may have become much more familiar with these sorts of concerns than with some of the other aspects of the task that I will be covering in this book. In fact I would argue that without a proper understanding of the full complexity of the leadership task, some of the knowledge about safety and child protection will never be fully implemented.

The other development of recent years is that the financing of care has shifted significantly, so that much residential care both in the UK and elsewhere is now provided by private companies, which in turn are often backed - and controlled - by 'big finance'. This situation has sometimes led to questions about the ethics and priorities involved (Toynbee 2014), especially where it is venture capitalists and hedge funds which have traded in such companies, sometimes leading to rapid shifts in policies and practice, sudden closures of units and inappropriate decisions about children's placements.

Meanwhile the research agenda has also expanded, exploring many details of care across this sector and increasingly concentrating on the 'outcomes' of care in the drive towards 'evidence-based practice'. Much of this research, it should be noted, has been government-driven rather than led by purely professional or academic concerns. See Fulcher and Ainsworth (2005) for a useful summary of these and other trends, and other texts such as Milligan & Stevens (2006), Smith (2009) and Kendrick (2007) for recent perspectives on residential child care policy and practice.

However, even though things have changed and evolved in many ways over these years, the approach to leadership that is taken in this book will be that the core of the task will remain the same whatever the changing context. Leaders do need to be aware of and engaged with the shifting sands of policy development, as well as seeking to influence further change, but their primary task is to provide the leadership that will enable their own unit or home to achieve its aims, and my aim here is to help leaders to think in depth and in detail about what is involved in this work.

**Outline**

The rest of this book is arranged as follows:

- **Chapter 1** begins with some personal reflections on the transition into a leadership role, before outlining some key ideas about leadership in residential child care practice - what it involves and how it operates at various levels.
- **Chapter 2** explores the nature of leadership, addressing such fundamental questions as 'Are leaders really necessary?' and 'What do leaders actually do?'
- **Chapter 3** examines the variety of roles that leaders may have to take on, and the tensions and challenges that may arise from having to do so much 'bridging' between different groups.
- In **Chapter 4** we will look at the detail of leading the team in particular, including the inter-personal dynamics between the leader and the team members individually and collectively, and at both conscious and unconscious levels.
- **Chapter 5** looks at the unconscious elements in the experience of leadership - the assumptions and psychological templates that we may each bring to our experience of leadership.
- **Chapter 6** sets the discussion in the context of values by examining the themes of 'Power, Prejudice and Dependency' in practice, and especially by drawing attention to the ways in which issues such

as gender and sexuality need to inform our consideration of leadership in contemporary practice.

- **Chapter 7** explores 'The Leader as a Person', beginning with the risks of isolation we have seen above, before returning to questions of authority and confidence.
- In the **Conclusion** we will think about 'What makes leadership work?', in other words what conditions and resources provide the best opportunities for high quality leadership in residential care and how can other systems support and contribute to this?

This is a lot of ground to cover in a relatively short space, but my hope is that the extensive use which I have made of practice examples will help to bring the discussion to life and so will promote further thought and reflection in the reader.

***Note:***

This book started life as a document commissioned for the National Centre for Excellence in Residential Child Care, which was then based at the National Children's Bureau in London. The original version was available as a pdf download from the NCB website, but it was never published in hard copy. The present version has been revised, updated and expanded for publication in this special hardback edition.

CHAPTER ONE

# Becoming a Leader

This chapter draws directly on my own experience of taking on a leadership role, which was not easy, and highlights some key issues about confidence and authority, proposing that leadership needs to be viewed as a 'process' rather than simply as a title or role.

## Leadership as a process

I began this book by saying that I will be taking a 'relationship-based' approach to the leadership task, by which I mean an approach which emphasizes the reality that in any 'care' organisation what will matter most of all is the quality of the human relationships at all levels (Ruch *et al.* 2010, Hennessey 2011). In the case of residential child care this means the relationships between the leader, the staff team and the young people, as well as the relationships of all of those inside the place with every-one on the outside, such as parents, siblings, teachers and social workers. It is a primary responsibility of leadership to monitor, influence and facilitate these relationships in support of the task of the organisation - in other words, to work closely and effectively with people at all levels to ensure that the work gets done and that people remain in good communication with each other despite any difficulties which may arise. In the context of child care, in which strong emotions may be evoked on all sides, this is by no means an easy task, and it requires skill, understanding and tolerance as well as a high level of self-knowledge.

What goes with this relationship-based approach is an emphasis on leadership as a process: an ongoing, evolving and interactive process, rather than a static role, as might be represented by an organisational chart showing the formal hierarchy. Leadership takes time: as with any other relationship or set of relationships, you grow into it through a transitional phase. In effect, you gradually *become* the role, and then as the relationships develop and grow further you can increasingly use these relationships (in the best sense) to work as effectively as you can; and then eventually you move on to another role, perhaps elsewhere.

It is especially important to bear in mind that last bit - the *moving on.* The truism that 'nobody is indispensable' should apply to leadership just as much as to any other role, and yet it is not uncommon to come across apparently good and effective leaders who have sought to make themselves indispensable by playing up the charismatic or 'transformational' aspects of their role. They begin to behave as if nobody else could ever make such a good job of leadership as themselves, only to ultimately fulfil their own prophecy when they leave and the place collapses or implodes, because the Dear Leader has undermined or sabotaged everyone else's own confidence. We often see this pattern unfold in political leadership and it is just as true in the professional world. It therefore behoves every leader to be mindful of their own temporary hold on the role and to avoid the temptation to become too much of a 'queen bee' or 'king-pin', and we will see some examples later of dominant or overbearing leaders who have eventually come unstuck.

**The Transition into Leadership**

The other - and more obvious - critical point in this 'process' model is the transition *into* leadership, which I have written about elsewhere (Ward 2002). This transition into really *becoming* a leader (as opposed to being simply appointed to the position) involves much negotiation and often testing out, sometimes directly and sometimes quite indirectly, as well as a considerable amount of trial and error on the part of the new leader.

New leaders have to establish their credibility in all parts of the organisation, and to find their authority at a personal level as well as at the 'given' level within the organisation. Since the leader is such a key figure in the life of the place, he or she is likely to attract strong feelings of many sorts, as we shall see throughout this book, and especially in terms of whether they will come to be seen as not only reliable, trustworthy and knowledgeable but also respectful of others and flexible in their outlook.

This is indeed a tall order, and it helps to explain why the transitional phase of the process may take some time: although it is certainly possible to make a good first impression, it may take much longer in reality to establish and develop meaningful relationships throughout the place. Colleagues and children alike will need to make up their own minds both individually and collectively about their new boss and perhaps test them in a variety of situations in order to establish the necessary trust. The interesting thing about the group care context, of course, is that so much of the work is done in public or semi-public. Everybody sees how the leader responds to a child in distress or acting defiantly, or to an 'awkward' staff member, and so everybody has plenty of evidence on which to base their judgement of their new leader. In particular they will be able to spot any mismatch between the leader's espoused philosophy of care and his or her actual behaviour. This may also be helpful in terms of the leader being seen to have 'feet of clay' and as sometimes having to struggle to cope with the demands of difficult situations or challenging individuals just as others do, despite being more senior or experienced.

The other thing about the public context is that a new leader may sometimes be tested out by one person or group as if on behalf of another, as we shall see below. For this reason there may often seem to be a 'performative' element in the way the leader responds to challenge in the early days of the transition, knowing full well that although reputations can take a long time to become fully established, they can also founder on the rocks with alarming speed. Being seen to cope well in an early crisis may turn out to be of lasting value, and it may be important to be aware that an interaction with one person or group may also be closely scrutinized by others.

To illustrate this discussion about transition I will offer a very personal account of my own experience. When I began my career as a leader in residential child care it was still the time of the 20-bed general purpose children's home, with a small army of domestic staff and a rather smaller troop of child care staff, some of whom lived on site and very few of whom were trained. The training situation has been slow to improve, although other things have changed significantly.

For me the process of getting established as a leader was a very difficult time. I was very young - in my mid-twenties, which really was much too young to have found myself in this role - and I was in some ways quite naive, although I did have social work training and quite a bit of relevant experience. Even though I had been a deputy elsewhere and had previously spent some difficult months as 'acting' in charge of another home, there were many things which I was simply not ready for when I was appointed as 'Superintendent', as the job was known in the 1980s. Some of the staff had been there for many years and knew the children inside out (it was a 'long-stay' home), and had weathered the storms of a period of great change. The previous boss and his wife (there were still married couples running children's homes at that time) had been in post for over ten years, and they were seen as highly successful in their work - indeed their fame had spread far and wide after a BBC TV documentary, *A Home Like Ours*, was made about the home.

However, as we have already seen, when such high-profile leaders eventually leave there is considerable risk of things falling apart. And sure enough when this couple left there had been a very unhappy appointment which had only lasted for a few months. This had been followed by a further period when the 'acting-up' role was held by the deputy - whom I experienced as a hard-bitten, cynical man, who would sabotage staff meetings by doing the crossword and muttering destructive comments under his breath. Some of the staff had become care-worn or 'burnt-out', which had left them insufficiently reflective of their task, although a few others were keen to make a new start and eventually we were also able to start making new appointments. Overall they were not a happy crew.

The gradual process of renewal enabled me to find my feet and establish some authority with the team, although I was learning that there is a big difference between being given authority from 'above' (i.e. being appointed to the role) and developing it from within - really believing it and feeling able to act and speak with sufficient authority. My first boss in my previous job had been an excellent model in this respect, and to some extent I probably modelled myself on him, although I still needed to find my own authentic way of holding this position: imitating someone else's style was never going to be enough to fulfil what was expected of me.

Over the coming months things gradually improved but I was still quite lacking in confidence. The children were aware of this and were naturally adept at making the tensions very evident by testing me out in front of other 'tougher' staff and kids. It felt like a trial of strength, in which I had to prove that I was hard enough to withstand anything that was thrown at me - quite literally so on some occasions. At the same time what I wanted to establish was something very different: I wanted to model a form of care in which positive and caring relationships would develop both between staff and children and within the staff team itself. This didn't seem too much to ask, as it was supposed to be a 'therapeutic' home, and yet it felt very difficult and even risky to try and establish such an ethos, especially after the prolonged period of disruption and loss which had preceded my arrival. There was a particular challenge involved in trying to lead such a change of ethos, because although what I wanted to establish was a co-operative and collaborative set of relationships, it felt like I might have to be very assertive and even pushy to establish it, which seemed paradoxical. Perhaps I was discovering how difficult it was to establish a new ethos or organisational culture, when so many things seemed to be standing in the way.

Meanwhile the domestic staff had their own views and had seen it all before. This long-established group of local women had lived through many changes of personnel as well as all their own crises. Many of them were old enough to be my mother, and one or two of them even perhaps my grandmother, so they were not usually pleased to be asked to do things by me. Indeed they greatly preferred running their own regime and schedules as they had always done, however inefficient and sometimes irrelevant this might seem to me (was it really necessary to polish the brass door-handles every day?) Where possible I delegated the management of the domestic staff to a female colleague, which was probably both rather a cop-out and sexist on my part, although there did seem to be a good rationale for it based on the reality that different tasks can often be best achieved by different people and that this factor needs to be taken into account in any delegating.

Two particular incidents of the testing and challenging which I endured, stick out in my mind.

**Example 1.1 The office**

There came a time when I felt that in order to establish myself more confidently I would need my own office, as until then I had had to share the general office not only with the secretary, but also with staff escaping for a coffee or cigarette or to find money from the petty cash tin, and sometimes with a wayward child hauled out of trouble to be spoken with. There was no space in the general office either for guaranteed privacy or for the sort of individual and team *thinking* which needed to happen. Although it was a large and rambling building, there was not much available room for an office anywhere near the heart of the action where I felt I needed to be, rather than tucked away at the end of a corridor, which would have been one option.

One space that I had my eye on was the 'sewing room', where the children's clothes were ironed, folded and mended (not washed, this was done in a different room). It was a pleasant enough little space whose only drawbacks were that it had bars on the window, perhaps left over from the time when the safe may have been kept in there, and that it was occupied at times by one or two of the domestic staff. Nevertheless I felt it was the best available option for my own office and I explained this to the domestics, found them another space, and set out about renovating and re-decorating it - and removing the bars. To have brought in a council decorator to do the job would probably have taken some years to organise and budget, so I decided I would have to do it myself. After a few days, when I was in there up a ladder with a paintbrush, the smallest and frailest of the domestic staff, Mollie, put her head round the door in an apparently friendly manner, saying "Ooh that's nice dear - you're a painter are you?" "Only in my spare time" I replied. "Very nice, dear" came the reply. Then there was a pause, followed by: "Hitler was a painter, you know", and she left, letting the door shut silently behind her. I received the message quite clearly: my search for *lebensraum* was not welcome, and would be resisted.

This was my introduction to the ambivalence which people felt towards leadership, especially when it had previously been missing or problematic: everybody knew it was necessary for everyone else, but they did not really want it to impinge directly on themselves. It was also a reminder that being the leader meant being a leader to *everyone* in the place, not just to the children and the child care staff.

The second incident in my introduction to the leadership role was more painful and even humiliating. Perhaps three months into the post I was still trying to establish real authority with the children, especially the ones who had lived there for some time before I had arrived (several years in some cases). Their lives had been dreadfully disrupted not only by the traumas in their original families but also by the more recent upheavals in the children's home. I knew all this and felt I understood it - and thought I understood why they needed to 'take it out' on the staff and especially on me in my role as the new figurehead.

**Example 1.2 Tears before bedtime.**

One winter's evening there was a sudden - though not unexpected - power-cut (this incident occurred during a time of nationwide political and industrial disruption), and this black-out led rapidly to pandemonium. The children were frightened, especially when one of the older boys grabbed one of the candles which we were having to use for lighting and tried to set fire to the curtains. In an atmosphere of panic and contagious anxiety, we decided to 'divide and rule' by taking the children in small groups to different parts of the house.

I took on the job of trying to contain a small group of the younger children who were by now in complete panic. I decided to bring them upstairs into a small 'quiet room' which was normally used for reading bedtime stories to the children, and I tried to encourage them to sit down and calm down. Instead they took this opportunity to vent all their pain and fear by attacking me, first verbally and then physically by throwing the reading-books at me. Although I shouted at them again to try to quieten them, this still had little effect. I decided it was best not to retaliate or to make things worse by losing my temper with them (though with hindsight that might have been the most appropriate thing to do), and I tried to stand my ground. But in truth I too was scared by now, and overwhelmed with the whole situation, and a tear appeared in my eye: I didn't actually break down in tears, but my distress and unhappiness was clearly showing. At this moment, all my idealism and optimism about what I might have been able to achieve in this place seemed to lie in ruins around me: I felt a failure and fully expected to lose my job within a few days.

As the lights eventually came back on, one of the younger boys looked at me and pointed to the tear still in the corner of my eye, initially with apparent triumph, although this soon turned to anxiety and perhaps guilt on his part, as he called out to the others that they had ‘made him cry’. For them there was something both appalling and fascinating about seeing this evidence of my distress, which so obviously mirrored their own. This only made me feel worse, of course, as I would far rather have concealed the evidence and indeed would have preferred not to have felt so upset in the first place. But there was also a raw and undeniable power in this situation: it seemed to signify that we had all reached 'rock bottom' together, and could only come back from there together. In fact order was soon restored, the children calmed down and the staff were able to re-group and re-establish themselves. As a leader I still felt something of a failure for a while, although in the long run I found I had gained new confidence from discovering that even the most difficult situation could be survived with everyone intact. I was also fortunate in being supported by excellent senior managers, who reassured me that having one difficult night did not mean that I was going to lose my job.

Some years later, and still in the same post, I wrote a short article, which has recently been reprinted (Ward 2014), based on my experiences during this period, in which I quoted among other things these lines from the ancient Chinese text the *Tao te Ching* (LaoTsu, 1972):

> High winds do not last all morning
> Heavy rain does not last all day.

I had first come across this text a few years earlier and ever since it had often served to remind me that all troubles and worries will eventually pass and that what is important is surviving and learning from experience.

I would hope that other leaders would not experience such a dramatic and even dangerous situation as I did, although many experienced child care leaders have told me of their own equivalent 'moments of truth' when all appeared to be lost, either in terms of their work with an individual or a group, or indeed with the whole enterprise. As I pointed out in the Introduction, a children's home can be a place in which very powerful emotions including fear and even despair will be felt, and this is something which both staff and leaders seem to have to experience at its greatest power if they are going to go on to really help the young people to face and overcome their own anxieties. Tears are to some extent an occupational hazard for those working in such places, although that does not make them any more comfortable when they do appear.

**The leader as figurehead?**

What I learned from incidents such as these was that what really mattered in my role as leader was not my qualification or university education, nor the books that I had read, but the immediate reality that I was now in the centre of a set of powerful human relationships in which my own responses and actions would be 'read' by others and scrutinized for both immediate and symbolic significance. It was becoming clear that these relationships were experienced (by all parties) not only at the practical and rational level, but also at the deeply emotional level of other important human relationships such as we normally experience only in our family or personal life. This would be true in any organisation, but in this particular kind of setting there was an especially powerful truth to the reality. I was somehow becoming the human figurehead, expected to lead and take all the knocks, and feeling that I had to inspire and motivate other people, even (or perhaps especially) when I was feeling anxious or depressed myself.

The notion of a figurehead is interesting: the leader does have to play this role at times, although it can be an isolating and risky one, and at times it can be quite an inappropriate metaphor. In the 'Valhalla' museum in the Tresco Abbey Gardens on the Isles of Scilly there is an impressive collection of ships' figureheads, which have mostly been salvaged from ships wrecked on the treacherous rocks around those islands. The figureheads have been restored and repainted magnificently, but they still show signs of the damage and battering which they routinely encounter right up at the front of the ship on the rockiest of voyages. However, the very fact that these figureheads taken from wrecked ships have eventually found themselves thus restored and displayed tells its own story: having a figurehead to take all the punishment is no guarantee of safe passage, either for the crew, the cargo or indeed the figurehead itself. Even though there may be some romantic appeal in the notion of being a 'figurehead' or 'heroic' leader, it may be better for new and aspiring leaders to avoid the self-delusion which may accompany such an image. It may in fact be better for the organisation that the leader is able to work through others to read signs of danger in advance and to help steer clear of them, rather than blundering on into them. I have seen more than one excellent residential unit crash heroically on to the metaphorical rocks partly because they had not spotted the rocks or realised how hazardous they were.

For most leaders, a more appropriate image than being a figurehead would probably be one of placing yourself at the heart of the system, ready and able to engage with people at whatever level is appropriate, whether with the children themselves, with their parents or other carers, or with the staff, as well as with the external contacts such as line management and other professionals. As a management system evolves around you, many of these contacts can be worked with and developed by others on your behalf as tasks and duties are delegated, but you are still accountable for the whole show, and that is what I was not fully prepared for when I took on the role. Perhaps you cannot be prepared for that in advance - you have to experience it at first hand, and discover what it feels like for yourself.

**A leadership team**

For me it all came together once I finally had a deputy with whom I could work in a genuine partnership of respect and trust, so that I was able to rely on him in what he said to me about the staff team and in what he said to them about me - not that he would always 'toe the line', but that his communications could be trusted and respected on all sides.

For many reasons the role of the deputy is an essential one in the leadership system. For example, it is probably inevitable that some of what a leader needs to do will be unpopular: asking people to face unpalatable truths about the future or about where their work may have gone wrong, or perhaps trying to introduce a change which people neither understand nor want. In these situations the relationship of respect and trust between leader and team can become strained as people may become resentful or undermining, or may retaliate with unthinking responses. What is needed is often a go-between, someone who is prepared to foster good will on both sides and to promote better communication when it is at risk of breaking down. This is where a good deputy is invaluable, to carry the spirit of good communication between all sides and to forestall the possibilities of mistrust and recrimination. In fact a good deputy is also a leader and uses many leadership skills, although perhaps in different ways from the appointed leader.

However, even a good deputy is not enough. These days although the number of residents in each home is smaller, the number of staff is generally much larger, and there is usually the need for a full leadership team within a home: the head, the deputy, and a number of team leaders or other senior staff. This arrangement allows for what is in effect a 'round table' approach to leadership, in which senior staff can consult and advise each other and build a genuine sense of shared responsibility into the system. The role of the leader within this team will still be one of leadership - small-group leadership, which requires another set of skills, including the ability to 'bring on' some people and to hold some back if they are treading on others' toes. But the overall effect will be to enable leadership to work in a more open and effective way.

I know of one large organisation, a residential school, in which the whole leadership team meets every morning at 9 o'clock after the children are in class, but before any other business of the day is done; and another in which the heads of several small units on the same site come together every day to confer and compare notes, under the leadership of the head of the whole organisation. Smaller homes may not have the resources for this sort of daily meeting, but its value is clear - it promotes what is sometimes known as 'distributed leadership' in which power is shared rather than excessively centralised on a single leader. We will see other examples of this approach in operation later in this book: its value is that it spreads the responsibilities of leadership amongst a senior team, although it in no way lessens the pivotal role of the formal leader.

**Summary**

Through looking at the important process of transition into a leadership role, the message of this first chapter has been that what a leader needs to do is to establish and develop a culture in which people can work together to get the work done, and in which they are clear about what their task is. I have shown how difficult this may be, and even though this book is focused on individual leadership, I have emphasized the value of establishing and working with a leadership team rather than attempting to be a 'figurehead leader'.

CHAPTER TWO

# Definitions and Theories of Leadership

Having begun by looking at the transition into leadership we will now back-track to look at what leaders actually do, and to consider some influential ideas about leadership. This will not be a compreh-ensive account, simply an introduction to some of the main issues and ideas that we will be using in the following chapters. Some of this may be familiar ground: we will look at ideas about influence and motivation and at change and vision, then examine the controversial idea of charismatic leadership, and consider its risks, setting this in the context of other common ideas about leadership 'style'. We will also look at the distinction often made between 'transactional' and 'transformational' leadership.

**Why are leaders necessary?**

Several research papers (e.g. Sinclair & Gibbs 1998) and inspection reports indicate clearly that good leadership is essential for successful residential care, and this makes sense at an intuitive level - but why should it be so? What is it that good leaders do which makes such a critical difference?

We can perhaps answer this more easily by first thinking about what might happen in the *absence* of leadership, if a children's home had no identifiable leader. While there might be some novelty to this situation at first, we could expect that things would soon become disorganised and even chaotic. In this scenario everybody might have their own idea about how things should be done but they would not necessarily co-ordinate their efforts with each other. People who did not conform with group norms or established practice might be neither challenged nor brought to account, or if so this might happen in an informal or unauthorised way. Staff might flounder in the absence of a sense of direction and purpose in their work and they might experience extra stress because they were lacking in support and guidance; and ultimately their motivation and loyalty might weaken because they felt less personally tied-in to the organisation.

In such circumstances the organisation would not hold together effectively for long, although it might soon happen that unofficial leaders would emerge. This would probably be no solution at all, however, because their authority would not be sanctioned or controlled from above, and probably not equally from all colleagues either. As differences emerged between different people's ways of doing things, time would need to be spent sorting out which approach was going to prevail, otherwise the young people would soon detect the differences in the expectations and responses of the various individuals or factions. The consequences for the young people might be serious, if they felt staff were either being inconsistent or were not really interested in them or engaged in helping them - and they might express their feelings through a variety of difficult and challenging behaviour, perhaps in an unspoken wish to provoke some resolution of the tensions.

In a sense the implied challenge of such behaviour would be to the staff, as if the young people were saying to them: 'Don't forget about us, we're important too, and we need looking after - and we need consistent care and attention'. Of course we do sometimes see the beginnings of such patterns emerging in many care settings, even those with the most effective leaders, but it is just this kind of scenario that a leader is often seeking to predict and prevent, or to resolve if it does start to develop.

What is perhaps most noticeable about the sort of scenario just described is that it is of course all about the *people* involved and how they all affect each other, and about the importance of the place being held together through good communication. This highlights the key role of leadership in working with people to get things done and the need to know when it is right to lead from the front, when to work alongside people and when to 'lead from behind', in the sense of stepping back and allowing others to begin developing their own leadership potential. One key skill of leadership therefore lies in this matter of knowing how to assess which particular approach may be most beneficial in any given situation - and since 'situations' are always evolving and each one is unique, this is a skill (sometimes known as 'situational leadership') which the leader is always needing to be ready with.

In fact it is surprisingly common for teams to find themselves either without a leader or with at least some lack of clarity as to who their leader really is or how much of a leader they are. Apart from those temporary situations in which a deputy or other senior person may find themselves 'acting up' into the role, there are other times when the leader of one place is asked to stand in temporarily in another, or when a sub-team is expected to be led by a temporary leader. At another level we do sometimes find leaders who are virtually absent, either because they are either ineffective or because they carry little or no real authority - in politics the phrase used is: 'in office but not in power'. This is a risky situation because of the dangers of the scenario described above.

What this discussion highlights is that a leaderless organisation is not viable for long, and that leaders do therefore play a critical role in holding organisations together, and especially in holding *people* together - and that this is just as true of children's homes as it is of banks, football teams and any other organisation. We will return later to this central theme of 'holding'.

**What do leaders do?**

If we stay for a moment with the image of the leaderless organisation but we now imagine a new leader walking in and taking over the leadership role - what would we expect them to actually do? One metaphor which is sometimes used is of the leader 'taking up the reins', as if the team was a team of horses to be harnessed together to pull the whole organisation along, watched, guided and steered by the leader. This is not altogether unhelpful as an image, despite its obvious limitations, because it does suggest that leadership involves encouragement, knowing the terrain and direction of travel, and choosing the best route, as well as harnessing the natural energies of the team. On the other hand this image does not really allow for the constant human interaction involved - the best team of horses simply follows orders as a group, whereas the most effective team of people will interact dynamically both amongst themselves and with the leader, and these interactions will contribute very significantly to the effectiveness of the whole team. So a leader trying to keep a child-care team 'in harness' would not last long either, and for the moment it might be better to return to our earlier metaphor of the team as a group of hill-walkers rather than as a bunch of animals!

***Organising***

The language that is most often used for the leadership role focuses on tasks such as influencing, motivating and organising. Of these activities it is easiest to specify the 'organising' tasks which leaders in children's homes actually carry out, including for example:

- bringing people together in meetings to discuss and agree upon what needs doing and how things are to be done,
- meeting with individuals and small groups of staff to supervise their work,
- meeting with young people and their families as part of their ongoing casework.

Essential though these planned meetings are, however, they only tell part of the story. On the one hand leaders also do a great deal of administrative work in support of the professional task, and some leaders become so preoccupied with this aspect of the work that they may end up neglecting the professional task. On the other hand leaders do also need to be visible and present in the unit, playing a significant role in the everyday life of the home, so that they will remain real to the young people and staff at all levels, rather than being seen as a distant authority figure. Finally, leaders also do a lot of work externally to the unit, meeting with senior managers and other professionals, often focusing on longer term policy and strategy. Some of this work will focus on future change and adaptation or on re-considering the task and direction of the unit, but a lot of it may be fairly humdrum in terms of meeting the expectations and requirements of the employing / funding organisation, such as budgetary and policy matters.

***Prioritising***

In the light of all these possible areas of work, an essential requirement of leaders is the ability to assess and prioritise their responsibilities, ensuring that they keep a reasonable balance between the various elements. Some tasks can be delegated, though none of them can safely be dismissed from the leader's mind. The leader therefore has to develop the capacity to keep all these areas of responsibility in mind and to continually review their own priorities and areas of focus.

**Example 2.1 Busy morning on the unit (part 1)**

It was a busy day in the adolescent unit: one of the young people had not gone to school because he was due to attend his case review in the unit that morning. He was feeling very tense and apprehensive about this meeting and had had a troubled night, keeping some of the other young people awake by shouting obscenities about his step-father. But there were also heating engineers in the building that morning, servicing the central heating system and making a lot of noise. Meanwhile a senior staff meeting to debate the implementation of a new policy on physical restraint was interrupted with the news that the cook had been taken ill and the agency replacement would not arrive until late morning. The staff were unsettled and the leader was working out which way to turn. ...

This is not an untypical day in the life of a residential unit, and even though there are no especially dramatic incidents, things are happening at many levels and it is not only the staff but also the leader who has to consider their priorities, making decisions as to what is most urgent, or most feasible. The leader's distinctive role is to take a 'reading' of the whole unfolding situation, including perhaps trying to reconcile competing or conflicting ideas about where their priority should lie, and to help the team to decide and act on these priorities. This all requires strategic and tactical thinking, leading to action which may be in the long-, medium- and/or short-term. It also requires an appreciation that the leader's view of any given situation may need to be deeper, broader and longer than the rest of the team may take, and so it may entail considering many different interpretations of the situation.

In Example 2.1, for instance, we might ask: should the leader propose that the first priority for the team must be attending to the needs of the individual troubled young person, or sticking to the important work on resolving policy – or should the leader perhaps go and cook lunch, and free up everyone else to get on with their scheduled work for the day? There is no single 'right answer', of course, and every leader will sometimes get it wrong and will need to learn from that experience. Working out the best answer on the day, through a combination of knowledge, intuition and sometimes improvisation, is part of what we mean by situational leadership.

### *Influencing and motivating*

The activities of organising and prioritising are relatively easy to specify, compared to the activities involved in influencing and motivating people. Here our focus changes from *what* leaders do to *how* they do it. Some of the 'influencing' role will be achieved through the process of modelling, in which the leader's effect is felt through an often-unspoken function of acting or speaking in a way, which will be experienced by the staff as a model for their own practice.

**Example 2.2 Busy morning on the unit (part 2)**

In the example above, one of the staff began to get agitated about the crisis in the kitchen and proposed that the policy meeting should be abandoned so that the staff could assist in preparing lunch. The leader, however, felt that this was an unnecessary disruption which would interfere with essential progress on the 'restraint' discussions, and found another solution to the missing cook by contacting a former employee who was willing to stand in at short notice to help out. In taking this course of action, the leader was thus modelling not only a spirit of adaptability and resourcefulness but also the importance of sticking to task rather than being blown off course by every new challenge.

The themes of influence and motivation are closely linked, and they are both affected by the degree and level at which the leader can engage with people. It is another truism that you will be unlikely to influence people much unless you can demonstrate that you are also open to being influenced by *them*, and that the most effective leaders are genuinely interested in hearing and using others' ideas, even if these are not always in full accord with their own. Another important ancient lesson in the power of influence comes from the parable of the sun and the wind competing to get the coat off a man's back. The wind howls and roars with rage, using what we might think of as 'heavy-end' influence techniques, but ultimately to no avail - the man just clings on to his coat all the more. And then the sun appears, and simply beams, but it does so with such warmth that the man discovers his own motivation to adjust his experience - and willingly removes the coat. This may sound a simplistic approach, but it is surprising how often (and how much) a little bit of genuine warmth and encouragement can motivate people - but also how some leaders never seem to think of trying this approach.

**Example 2.3 George and the chocolate brownies**

During a 'group supervision' meeting involving a number of heads of residential homes, one experienced leader, George, was complaining extensively that his staff team seemed unwilling or unable to 'go the extra mile' for the children. They apparently preferred to stick rigidly to their job descriptions, which often seemed to leave the young people feeling left out and unloved, which in turn would often lead to bad behaviour. The examples that he gave certainly seemed to support his view of the staff.

However, another leader in this discussion group thought it sounded as if George's staff team might have felt rather undervalued and emotionally depleted themselves, leaving them feeling that they had no more to give. It was suggested that they felt in some way 'unloved' by the organisation as a whole and even by George in particular - and that he might surprise and influence them by rewarding them in some way rather than always criticising them. At the next meeting George reported back to this group that he had brought in a plate of chocolate brownies for the next staff meeting, and consciously aimed to be much more warm and 'giving' to his staff. He had acknowledged to the staff that he may have taken too critical a stance towards them, and opened up the whole area for discussion. While one or two had viewed this turnaround suspiciously, others had responded warmly in turn and the atmosphere in the home had indeed begun to loosen up and warm up.

This example is not intended to suggest a simplistic connection between feeding one's staff and providing good leadership, but to hint that there are many ways to seek to influence people, and many ways in which the personal style of the leader may either support or inhibit the relational atmosphere of the whole place. In this case George reflected later in the discussion group that he now realised he had become somewhat too much of a 'stern parent' towards his team. This had probably contributed to the staff themselves offering a rather negative and withholding quality of care, which, in turn, had led to the young people's own negative behaviour.

## Change and vision

As we have already seen, an important component in leadership is the ability to envisage change and improvement, and to promote ways of achieving such change.

In every organisation there is constant change: for example, new people, new events and new policies. In residential care organisations there will be new referrals, admissions and departures, and unexpected events and crises, as well as the changes in the external world, which may affect the *type* of new referral, or the *way* in which referrals will come or will need to be handled. At another level there will occasionally be larger-scale changes, which may even affect the continued existence of the unit because of political or economic shifts, which affect policy. Change is not only externally-driven, however: it also comes from within, and most leaders will want to introduce their own changes at various levels, perhaps to improve the service or to develop some aspect of practice, or they may also want to encourage colleagues to propose and initiate change.

Since all this change is likely to impact upon the team and its work in many ways, the role of the leader will be to promote the best outcome of change, which will often depend on anticipating and preparing for change, and adjusting its demands in order to fit in with current practice and concerns. This will also involve supporting people through the process of change, which does not always run smoothly and which often requires individuals to adjust their practice and sometimes their dearly-held beliefs. Working with change often involves focusing on the future without ignoring either current realities or lessons from the past.

This focus on the future is sometimes referred to in the leadership literature as 'vision', although this is not necessarily a helpful metaphor if it is taken to imply that it is *only* the leader who needs vision. When the literature talks about 'vision' in leadership the impression is sometimes created that this vision will somehow emanate almost mystically from the leader and that in a blinding flash the veils of ignorance or confusion will then be lifted from everyone's eyes.

Nothing could be further from the truth. What 'vision' really involves in this context is the ability to help *other* people to see what needs doing and why, and together to 'envisage' the future. This may involve casting the collective organisational mind forward to imagine how the organisation or unit needs to develop, or where it needs to change and adapt, while simultaneously working with others to check out that vision. It may also involve consulting other people for their own vision and sometimes working together towards a workable compromise on whatever approach seems most likely to work. If it is only the leader who has the vision, everyone else may be blinded or prevented from seeing - somehow the leader needs to work with the team inside and out to share and develop the vision.

**Example 2.4 Working towards change**

In a small long-stay unit for adolescents, a proposal was put forward from head office to increase the occupancy by two beds, which would involve considerable building work and an increase in staffing levels. At first this proposal met with resistance both from staff and from the existing residents, who felt that the disruption involved would be destructive of what had come to feel like a safe and sheltered environment.

The leader initially worked with each group separately, staff and residents, feeling that the anxieties of the two groups were becoming conflated and almost 'feeding off each other'. This tactic was quite successful in defusing the great anxiety which had been building up, and the leader was also able to offer a genuine sense of optimism about the likely outcomes of the proposed change, and remained quietly confident though without putting too much pressure on others to 'share the vision'. As time moved on, each group, both adults and young people, began to recognise the possibility of positive outcomes from the change, and started working more constructively towards the change which they could now envisage as positive.

Leaders therefore need to be confident and constructive with change, neither resisting it because it upsets a smooth operation nor always looking for further change in a restless search for constant 'improvement'. This requires an appreciation of the need for both equilibrium and dynamism. In fact, even standing still (or 'stabilisation') is sometimes a priority in its own right, and one which requires considerable effort and determination: providing stability in turbulent times can be a real and valuable achievement.

**Leadership Style**

Much has been written about leadership style, often with the implication that if a leader can just come up with the 'right' style, all will be well. In fact this assumption is now largely discredited, mostly because of the huge range of variables in any organisation – the diverse personalities in any team, the broader social and organisational context in which the team is located, and so on. At the same time it is clear that at the far ends of the spectrum there are certainly 'wrong' styles: outright arrogance is never appropriate, and an extreme laissez-faire approach risks rapidly degenerating into the 'ineffective leader' or 'emotionally-absent' patterns we saw earlier.

Common sense also tells us that the same leader may not be equally effective in different settings - we only have to look at the variable fortunes of football managers to learn that lesson. The hearty or bombastic approach which worked in one team in a lower division may turn out to be completely ineffective with a team of inspired but arrogant superstars in a higher league, whereas the 'inspirational' leader who was able to bring out the best in a close-knit successful team may struggle to conjure the same effect in a divided or depressed team which has lived through an apparently never-ending string of defeats.

At the same time it is undeniable that personality or leadership style is *one* of the resources which a leader has to deploy. What effective leaders do is to match their style to the situation as it evolves: identifying, for example, when the team might benefit from an assertive or even confrontational approach and when it may be better to stand back a bit, tolerating difference and waiting for consensus or understanding to emerge. To work in this way requires genuine confidence and maturity, and depends upon the leader not only reading the situation well, but also knowing him- or herself well enough to be able to adjust their approach as necessary.

As we saw in the case of George and his retreat into an ungiving and demanding approach (Example 2.3, pp. 47-8), what the leader needs most of all is the ability to recognise the ways in which the emotional atmosphere of the unit may be influenced by his or her own style of relating, and the ability to seek and act upon feedback about how that style may be perceived by others. George was initially resistant to the feedback offered to him in the supervision group, but on further reflection he was able to recognise what was going on and then to take the personal risk of changing his approach.

Working in this way is similar to the idea of the 'use of self' in professional practice, which involves knowing your strengths and weaknesses and being able to draw upon those aspects of your personality which match what the situation demands (Ward, 2010).

It is also important that the leader should not be allowed to develop an over-powerful self-belief, and that reality-checks should always be built in. Some of this can be achieved through effective line-management and supervision systems, but because these are usually all part of the same organisational structure there is sometimes a risk that they will not be sufficiently objective. The leader should therefore also have regular consultation with an external person who can provide a foil and check against whatever delusions they may start to evolve. We will return to this theme in a later chapter.

### *Charisma*

In the context of leadership styles, the literature also frequently refers to the quality of charisma in leadership, and this has often been seen as either an essential or a highly risky aspect of the role. If by 'charisma' we mean the personal qualities needed to inspire and encourage people, to lead by example and provide motivational leadership, then some element of this is essential, because without it the personal bonds between members and leaders will not be formed. A leader who cannot inspire or even really encourage people will not get far, as we have seen, and in turn the quality of the work with the young people will probably remain dull and unresponsive. But if charisma tips over into arrogance, or into overweening self-belief and the arbitrary and self-justifying exercise of personal power, then of course it is dangerous (Hinshelwood 1990). Some of the most problematic situations in residential settings, just as in other organisations, have stemmed from the effects of the unchecked power of a charismatic leader.

Charisma is an elusive concept to pin down, and it turns out to have political and cultural 'baggage', as I learned during a consultancy visit to Russia which I undertook with a colleague in the early 1990s, when we had great difficulty in finding an agreed translation of this term when discussing leadership styles in residential services. From our own Western perspective our reference point for a charismatic political leader was their then-president Mikhail Gorbachev. He was perceived from the West as highly charismatic in the sense of having charm, drive and the ability to inspire people, although it turned out that despite these qualities, which they viewed as superficial or hypocritical, he was despised and distrusted by most ordinary Russians. Charismatic figures in UK politics are similar: adored by some and loathed by others, hugely forceful personalities who can sometimes exercise enormous power, even over those who oppose their views. Charisma, then, is not a straightforward or objective quality, and it may sometimes refer more to a behaviour pattern driven by personal motives than to a consciously adopted 'leadership style'.

**Example 2.5 Gary the omnipresent leader**

In one residential unit the leader, Gary, was always on duty, frequently working unexpected extra hours on an evening shift and at weekends. He was undoubtedly gifted in communication with young people, and if there was trouble brewing in a group he was often able to cajole them instead into a game of snooker or simply a chat over coffee. However,

> this was not always helpful for the other staff, who sometimes felt by-passed by Gary and even deskilled as his easy-going charm did not resolve tensions so much as postpone them until after he had left the building (equally unpredictably) - whereupon any submerged difficulties between the young people would re-surface, perhaps late in the evening when everyone was tired and the conflicts might be harder to resolve.

In this example, Gary's personal style risked undermining other team members and making their work in some respects harder. People found it hard to challenge Gary because his persona was so much built around being 'the nice guy', and 'everybody's friend'. It was only in the aftermath of one particular late-night incident in which a young person became violent towards another staff member that people felt more able to challenge Gary's leadership style. After some subsequent developmental work in the team, facilitated by an external trainer, the dynamics shifted very positively. Gary now began to focus his efforts more on supporting and developing the staff instead of feeling he needed to work directly with the young people so much. It turned out (as is often the case) that underlying Gary's apparent 'charisma' was a greater anxiety than anyone had previously realised about his own ability to lead the team and develop their abilities.

This had led him to prefer what felt to him like the 'safer ground' of direct work with the young people, perhaps in the hope that his colleagues would pick up some of his undeniable ability in that field. But far from picking it up, they had come to resent his approach: again what was temporarily missing was the leader's awareness of how his own style was actually being perceived, and again what led to change was carefully-managed feedback from an external advisor.

### *Transactional and Transformational Leadership*

A more recent concept and one which has become quite influential is the distinction between two styles of leadership characterised as the transactional and the transformational. These two are sometimes pitted against each other, with the message that the latter is the preferred model, although it is clear that any organisation needs both. Transactional leadership is usually seen as more concerned with structures, targets and systems - indeed Lawler (2006) equates it with the more traditional concerns of 'management', compared with the more person-focused concerns of leadership.

The concept of Transformational Leadership, on the other hand, originated in the works of US writers James Burns and later Bernard Bass. This approach tends to emphasize the moral element of leadership by moving beyond simply getting people to do what you want them to do in the way you want them to do it, and *transcending* everyday needs and expectations by aiming at higher or deeper goals. This is quite close to what is sometimes called the 'vision thing', and it does draw attention to the leadership role of inspiring people to think and plan beyond the immediate and the everyday, as well as to the techniques of personal influence and motivation often based on consciously acquired aspects of 'leadership style'.

While there is clearly a lot to be said for the motivational and inspirational elements of leadership that the transformational model promotes, on further reflection we may find that similar hazards may attend the transformational leader that we saw in the case of charismatic leadership. These might include excessive self-importance and self-belief on the part of the leader, and the building of a personal empire in which staff are (perhaps unwittingly) encouraged to become overly dependent on the personal approach of the leader.

In the case of charismatic or transformational leadership, then, what is needed is that vital extra element of self-monitoring and self-awareness (preferably supported by external consultation), so that the leader will realise the risks as well as the benefits of any given leadership style. The leader therefore needs the ability to select appropriately from within a range of styles and approaches and to tailor them to the evolving situation.

### Leadership and 'followership'

We have already seen that the relationship-based approach used in this book emphasises the interactional aspects of the role of leadership, and promotes an awareness on the part of leaders of the quality of communication which they can establish between themselves and their teams. Some of the literature focuses directly on what are seen as the complementary roles of leader and follower, and considers the implications for the latter, including discussions of what constitutes good 'followership'. There is a certain value to this approach, which may cause us to re-examine the very term 'leadership': after all, if someone is the 'leader' then others must be the 'led' or the 'followers'.

There is perhaps also an implication that leaders need to evoke in their staff a willingness to be led, to trust enough to follow, and trust is certainly an essential ingredient. However, 'followership' is a strange concept: I am not convinced that many of us would really like to think of ourselves as being 'good followers', and it would not normally be taken as a complement to be said to be 'good followership material' in the sense that being 'good leadership material' definitely has a positive ring. We like to think of ourselves as autonomous adults, even though we will agree where necessary to work with the consensus and collaborate with others to achieve shared goals, usually under the leadership of a key individual. That is what teamwork is all about, but if 'followership' does have connotations of unquestioning compliance with a leader's wishes, then it cannot be an appropriate model. (Or am I revealing here that I have never been very good at complying with others' wishes?) Perhaps a more positive construction would be to think in terms of being thought a 'good team player' and to have team membership skills (Collins & Bruce 1984). So, rather than followership, we can now think in terms of the skills of collaborative working, the ability to both give and take support, and the ability to always work with the rest of the team and its task in mind.

## Summary

In this chapter we have explored some of the basic ideas about leadership - why leaders are necessary, what they actually do, and how they do it. We have considered the question of leadership style and in particular we have debated the merits of 'charismatic' and 'transformational' leadership styles. The main message from this chapter is that leadership is a complex and demanding task, which requires the ability to operate at many levels, as well as self-awareness and the ability to move between these levels as priorities shift and circumstances unfold, and to adjust one's way of working accordingly.

CHAPTER THREE

# Leadership: Boundaries And Roles

In this chapter we will be thinking in more detail about the activities of the leader, especially in relation to the roles which he or she plays and the boundaries which the leader has to constantly monitor and negotiate. We will look at how the leader needs to place him or herself in relation to these boundaries. By 'boundaries' I mean the distinctions between people's roles: both their own clarity about what they themselves should or should not be doing, and their clarity about each others' roles. In the fluidity and mêlée of everyday life in residential care there are many ways in which these roles and responsibilities can become blurred or muddled - often without people realising it - and the leader's role is to enable all staff to keep a sharp eye on these distinctions, but without going to the opposite extreme and creating a rigid and inflexible system.

**The myth of the hero-leader**

What is a leader and how would you spot one if you saw them in the street? One popular image of the leader is perhaps of a tall, dynamic figure up at the front of a battle line, leading the charge, issuing orders and never looking back. This is what is sometimes known as the 'hero-leader', someone who is at the centre of everything and who probably has a finger in every pie, a view on every problem and a solution to every challenge, and who - in extreme cases - probably has something to say on the details of every smallest part of the organisation and its work. We have all met them! It is an image that appeals to the popular imagination, perhaps because it also plays into semi-mythical images such as wartime leaders and epic heroes as well as into the psychological model of the idealised parental figure, and especially the stereotypical father figure.

This is in one sense a comforting image, conjuring up the notion that there will be someone in every organisation who will know everything and be able to resolve every difficulty, but who will also actively 'lead' the people into the future, perhaps even with the biblical connotations of 'leading them to the promised land'. At the same time, however, this is an unrealistic and out-dated image, and one that can only lead to frustration and disappointment if followed too closely. Nowadays the image of an all-powerful, all-knowing leader has uncomfortable echoes of totalitarian systems, and yet it is never far from the corporate or public imaginations, as we have seen in the media in recent years with television programmes which glorify the role of powerful (and often arrogant) business leaders. In reality, in most contemporary western organisations, a leader who seeks or claims to know everything and have all the answers will probably not last long.

We are now much more familiar with a model in which the leader is not only a director of operations but also a facilitator of others, and especially one who aims to work *with and through others* in order to get things done and to achieve the organisation's goals.

As we have already seen, any human service organisation such as a children's home involves a complex interplay between many individuals, groups and groupings, between those on the 'inside' of the organisation and those on the outside, i.e. both those for whom the organisation provides a service (the young people, their families) and those on whose behalf it does so (the agency and the authorities which sanction its operation, and ultimately society as a whole). The role of the leader will be to work together with all these groups and to enable them to work with each other, so that the agreed aims can be achieved.

What the leader needs to know and work with, therefore, is not so much the details of every far-flung part of the operation (though there are times when leaders do need this detailed information), but the size, shape and concerns of each of the groupings, and how they all relate with each other as well as with the 'whole'.

In this model of the organisation as a collection of inter-related groups, the leadership role is no longer one of commanding the troops and enforcing the law but of articulating the connections and facilitating the relationships between the various groupings.

**Example 3.1 Tension between two units**

In a children's home with an education unit attached, tensions began to emerge between the residential care team and the teaching staff as to whose methods of handling difficult behaviour in the children were 'right'. Despite clear policies and guidelines, the tension between the two staff groups increased as children began to exploit the inconsistencies which they sensed, and what had begun as subtle differences of emphasis and style gradually became almost polar opposites, as each 'side' became entrenched in their respective positions. Things only began to improve after the heads of the home and school sections jointly agreed to set up a series of regular meetings between the two groups, where people could air their differences, recognise their shared aims and find better ways of collaborating.

In the above example, as in most of the examples in this book, the way forward from difficulty was for the leader(s) not to instruct people to change their ways but instead to identify the best way to promote and facilitate good communication and mutual understanding, and to bring the relevant people together to work on that way forward. This will not always be easy, of course, and my aim in offering examples such as this one is not to suggest that quick solutions to conflict can always be found, but to suggest that the leader's task is often one of enabling other people to work together to resolve the difficulties which they find themselves in, rather than one of 'solving' problems him- or herself. Equally, this is not to imply that leaders do not have to be decisive and authoritative at times, but to confirm that the best starting point is often to enable others to articulate their own positions and to use their own authority.

It is open and clear communication that is the hallmark of good leadership and this translates into practice throughout the organisation. If there is conflict, the first priority is usually to attend to distorted or blocked communication so that others can deal with the things which they have personal knowledge of rather than for the leader to try and fix something of which he or she may have no direct knowledge. In this way everyone stays more or less with the boundaries of their own role, rather than sliding into others' areas of responsibility.

### Authority

Authority operates at more than one level: on the one hand there is the authority given by the formal role and which we exercise on behalf of the organisation, and on the other hand there is the personal authority which we achieve within our role by means of the process of relationship and negotiation which is the subject of this book. It is perfectly possible to have one without the other - to hold the formal role without the personal effectiveness, or *vice versa* to rise above the constraints of a muddled organisation and nevertheless offer genuine leadership. The best position, of course, is to combine the authority of the role with the ability to lead through relationship, without over-relying on either aspect.

Equally the use of authority is something of a sober responsibility - leaders would do well to remember that their very position gives them authority and that as we have seen elsewhere in this book they will be seen and experienced by others as having power at many levels. They do not generally need to add to this situation by attempting to remind people of their power or to insist on their 'right to manage', or on their 'right to be shown respect'. The paradox of leadership is that it may often be better achieved by not insisting on it:

**Example 3.2 Adrian and the coffee pot**

I learned very early on in my residential career that you can't *make* anybody do anything. You can persuade, encourage, cajole, inspire or implore, but you can't actually make it happen - whether it is a reluctant teenager who needs to curtail their behaviour or a resistant staff member who doesn't want to work in a particular way. You can insist upon compliance, but that is not the point, and often the more that you do so, the less compliance you will actually evoke - as I learned to my embarrassment when I was a very young acting-up 'officer-in-charge' and I ordered one of the junior staff to refill a coffee pot. She refused but I stood my ground ... and before long, and much to the amusement of the other staff, I was told where the coffee pot could be put, and it would not have been a comfortable experience.

## Boundaries

In order both to exert personal authority and to facilitate others' problem-solving abilities, leaders need to give careful thought to their position with regard to others. In this respect a useful way of thinking about the leadership role is to focus on the concept of boundaries, because it is across these demarcation lines between all the various individuals and groupings that the connections and relationships have to be managed.

From this perspective, leadership can now be seen as a role involving continual attention to boundaries - not only the literal boundaries between the residential unit and the neighbourhood, but also the metaphorical boundaries between the unit and the rest of the organisation to which it belongs, as well as the lines of distinction between all the different groups of people involved - the staff team, the management team, the young people and unit as a whole, and the families as well as the other professionals. The leader is continually monitoring the 'traffic' across these boundaries: where are the tensions, and what are the perceptions which each group holds both of themselves and of the others - as well as of the leader?

**Example 3.3 Disturbance beyond the boundary**

One night there was a minor disturbance outside a small residential home for adolescents, involving a lot of shouting and swearing. This had eventually led to the police being called, although no damage was done and it turned out that the young people in the home were not involved. Nevertheless the next morning the manager personally visited some of the neighbours to metaphorically 'mend fences' which had not actually been broken, although not surprisingly the young people in the home had come under suspicion of causing or provoking the incident.

In fact the leader often has to step in and out of role in these different groups, and to represent one group to another, sometimes over apparently trivial issues, but at other times over much more critical matters. This requires flexibility and the ability to negotiate and mediate between conflicting interests. It is not only a question of negotiation, though, but also of being seen by the various groups as having power and authority - and working appropriately with the feelings which this may lead to, as well as sometimes bringing groups together to do their own negotiating. In the above example, if the disturbance *had* been caused by the young people in the home, there may well have needed to be a series of meetings both within the home and between neighbours, staff and young people, in an effort to restore relationships to a workable level, and with the leader perhaps playing a 'bridging' or mediating role as described below.

Often the leader will also need to represent the place beyond these boundaries and outside the agency, or to defend its task and its boundaries in matters of policy and planning, ensuring that these are defined in such a way as to fit well and match the supply-and-demand chain. This will sometimes involve reminding the outside world of the existence and needs of the unit, and promoting its image if necessary.

**Example 3.4 Bringing a manager on site**

Jenny was the head of a local authority children's home which was coming under pressure because of a fall-off in referrals. When she heard that the future of the home was to be discussed at a senior management meeting she requested an individual meeting with one of these managers, and proposed that this meeting should be held at the home itself, to remind her of both the potential and the previous effective work in the place, and hoping thereby to influence her into becoming more of an advocate for the place. The manager came at the end of 'office hours' one day, when the young people were in the building and making a variety of demands which the staff were struggling to meet, and she was impressed at the staff's ability to respond positively to what were sometimes very challenging demands. There was no tangible outcome from this meeting but at the very least an effective rapport was established with this senior manager which may have played a useful role in the subsequent discussions of the home and its potential.

### The *place* of leadership

If leaders do have to pay continual attention to these boundaries, the question arises as to where they should seek to position themselves in relation to all these various groups - perhaps as a go-between or channel of communication, or maybe as a figurehead for them to aim at (although we have already seen in Chapter One that being a figurehead may be a dangerous role)?

It has been argued in particular that the role of the leader is to stay on the boundary between the inside and outside of the unit, holding and 'containing' what is within but also watching carefully what is going on externally - this is where the figure of Janus, the Roman god with two faces who guarded doorways, comes in. As we saw earlier, this may be an uncomfortable position, because it may leave the leader in an exposed and even isolated position, because if you spend *all* your time on the boundary there is an implication that you do not really belong either on the inside or the outside. We have all seen leaders who are out of touch with their team and command little respect, and who can therefore effect little change. This may happen if they are too closely identified with a 'head office' perspective, but equally it may happen if they just feel too anxious in the role, and retreat into a personal comfort zone - or into a single role, such as always just seeking to enforce regulations or perhaps trying to be a kindly parental figure. They may imagine such a role will keep them protected from the complexity of the demands and buffered from the impact of daily events in the unit, although in reality it may well prevent them from being truly effective.

**Bridging role**

When leaders aim to position themselves on the boundary, they therefore need to be careful not to use this position as a defence against involvement with either side. Being on the boundary in this case may mean playing a 'bridging role': helping people on each side to appreciate each other's position, or to clarify their own position, but with firmly rooted connections to both banks of the river.

They will also need to be aware of the risk in this position of being unwittingly 'set up' for conflict. If there are tensions between inside and outside, or between staff and young people, then putting yourself in the middle of it all may be the toughest position of all, 'between a rock and a hard place', as the saying goes. An effective leader can have considerable impact in this bridging role, especially if they are genuinely sensitive to the feelings on all sides, but it may be a stressful position to inhabit, where all the tensions in the system are felt most powerfully. As a leader this may be where your talents are best used but it may also be where your pain is most felt, either because you have a personal 'resonance' for a particular type of emotion, or because you feel most at home with certain patterns of interaction. For example, some people appear to find satisfaction in a leadership role just *because* it enables them to remain unattached - and this is not necessarily a healthy situation. Once again the key is to develop awareness at many levels, including self-awareness.

**Working with blurred boundaries**

One of the most important qualities of effective leadership is therefore the ability to establish and maintain clear boundaries - being exactly clear as to who should be doing what and why, who is *leading* what, as well as being clear about the nature and quality of these relationships. Part of what leaders are required to do is to help everyone else be clear about their roles, including not only what they are supposed to do but also what they are *not* expected to do, their 'cut-off points'. This is not always as straightforward as it sounds: at times there can be many pressures to blur the boundaries, and indeed some occasions when over-rigid boundaries are not helpful. These pressures may be subtle as well as overt, and they are very often connected with anxiety, which is what leaders then have to address.

**Example 3.5 Mike the too-chummy worker**

As head of the unit, Anne was concerned that Mike, a new member of her staff, was giving mixed messages to the young people by being too 'chummy' with them at times but then at other times having to suddenly switch roles and revert to a very controlling role when he realised that they were getting out of hand. Anne felt that Mike's over-familiar persona, as if he was implying to the young people 'we're all teenagers together', was probably done to try and make himself feel more comfortable, although it actually made the young people less comfortable because they didn't know where they stood with him.

However, although she was aware of the problem, Anne liked Mike (after all, she liked teenagers!) and she felt he was a promising prospect for promotion, so as time went on she didn't do enough to discourage his overtures to the young people, which she preferred to view as simply his ability to establish positive relationships. In effect she was colluding with him, because she didn't feel comfortable herself in drawing this particular boundary. Thus an important bit of leadership was missing, and there was also something odd happening in the way that Annie seemed to be unconsciously repeating in her handling of Mike that same lack of clarity which he was displaying in his relationships with the young people ... and all the while, she suspected that sooner or later she would have to call him to order, even though when challenged by her own supervisor to do so she was still reluctant.

What this situation confirmed was that collusion and the blurring of boundaries is unhelpful not only in everyday practice but also in leadership. Collusion (which literally means 'playing along with') can become corrosive, taking us off-task or even anti-task, but it can also be contagious: as we have just seen, if one person colludes, then others may find themselves doing so too. There is a style of leadership that might be called 'Arm round the Shoulder' in which the leader may imply that 'we're all pals together', but which is unrealistic because it denies and seeks to blur the necessary power and authority elements in the relationship. When the power finally has to be re-asserted, the denial is revealed and everyone may feel shocked by the sudden reversion to what should have been in place originally. This is not to say, of course, that leaders should never relax and relate more informally with their staff, but that they will still need to remain conscious of their role and responsibilities, and to occasionally remind others of these. In fact in most organisations the pretence on anyone's part that 'Everyone is equal' in power or status is likely to be an unreal and confusing message.

If we are to apply a 'relationship-based' approach to leadership, then we will have to pay attention to the currency and means of conduct for these relationships – the personal qualities of the leader, their levels of self-awareness and their ability to monitor and deploy the self at all levels of practice. This relates to what is sometimes called emotional intelligence (Howe 2008), and it requires considerable skill and awareness which will in turn benefit from training and ongoing supervision. It involves learning in depth about the ways in which emotions may 'fly around' in organisations, sometimes leading to people experiencing unaccountably strong reactions to each other and not knowing how to even begin to address these. The leader, too, risks getting caught up in this potential maelstrom, and this is where the additional help of an external staff consultant can be vital.

**Example 3.6 Kate and turning a blind eye**

I was supervising Kate, a therapist who was acting as staff group consultant to a facility for a large group of young offenders. On one occasion she told me that the staff had told her in passing that on the evening shifts a 'blind eye' was being turned to the fact that some of the young people were sometimes indulging in bullying behaviour and demanding money from younger residents. This was a situation that could clearly put some of the more vulnerable residents at risk of being exploited by others, and yet somehow it had evolved into a form of practice that nobody challenged. Kate reported this to me in passing while relating some other incident and I registered some surprise but again somehow passed it by. It was only when I was mentioning this detail to

> my own supervisor (again 'in passing') that the buck finally stopped and we recognised together that there was collusion going on, and that this situation needed to be halted and challenged. Subsequently I went back to Kate and pointed out the seriousness of the situation, reminding her of her responsibility to address it directly.

In this situation an underlying anxiety about the effects of the bullying had built up and spread (perhaps unconsciously) throughout the staff team, but nobody had been able to break the cycle of denial and collusion until it eventually reached an external person who called a halt. Once this was done, it was relatively straightforward to take it back into the organisation and address the issue directly, bringing a sense of relief at every level that the situation was back under control.

**Risks in boundary management**

Just as we approached the role of leadership by imagining an organisation without a leader, we can perhaps appreciate the need for boundaries more clearly if we explore some of the ways in which boundaries may be *mis*managed - and the consequences. In the case of Anne and Mike (Example 3.5, pp74-5), there was a sort of collusion between the leader and a staff member which perpetuated unhelpful practice. There may also be collusion in the other direction, between the leader and senior managers, so that the leader becomes over-identified with the more external position of overseeing and perhaps controlling the place, rather than staying on the boundary and mediating between the external and internal.

**Example 3.7 The absentee manager**

The leader of a unit preparing children for foster care was invited to join a senior planning team project group that was exploring future policy in the agency. She found this role stimulating and somewhat more comfortable than everyday life in the unit, and after the project group finished she continued visiting Headquarters on frequent occasions and became less present in the home and eventually she began to be perceived by the care staff as an 'absentee manager'. She had stepped too far outside the external boundary and was no longer an effective leader within the unit itself.

Equally some organisations create their own boundary difficulties through the organisational structures which they devise. One child care charity established a children's home with a top-heavy structure of three deputy heads and four team leaders in a relatively small staff team. Too many people were competing to lead the team, with the result that it was like an over-crowded elevator: no-one could turn around or even stand comfortably in their own place. It all became over-heated and there was continual argument as to who was in charge of what - much of which could have been prevented by having fewer people striving to be in charge in the first place. I became involved as staff team consultant and spent some time helping the team to untangle the complicated tensions which this arrangement had fed, before assisting the senior managers to devise a simpler slimmed-down structure in which people could be clearer about their own and each others' responsibilities. The whole team soon came to value the new arrangements as people now had a much clearer view about who to turn to in any given situation.

**Summary**

This chapter has introduced the important concept of boundaries and has explored why and how boundaries may sometimes become blurred or may even be denied. We have also looked at the role of the leader with respect to boundaries and the idea of the leader performing a 'bridging' role between different groupings, and being able to work *on* the boundary rather than being pulled to one side or another.

CHAPTER FOUR

# Working In The Everyday: The Leader And The Team

Having looked at the role of leadership and at some of the issues around boundaries, we will now examine the interactions between the leader and the team, especially bearing in mind the nature of the team's work with the reality of the emotional situation facing the young people.

## The nature of the team's work

I want to return to my comments in the Introduction (p.9):

> 'A children's home could be described as a small and intense human organisation, providing care and support for separated children, and focused on addressing the pain and challenges which they face and supporting them towards some resolution of the crisis in their lives.'

It is essential to keep this reality in mind, especially because there is sometimes an element of 'defensive' thinking which creeps in to policy and practice with children in residential care. This sometimes takes the form of arguing that 'all these children need is good ordinary care' rather than any specifically 'therapeutic' help. While nobody would argue against good ordinary care, we must remember that the extreme turmoil and disruption which most of these young people have experienced earlier in their lives is likely to have left them with many troubled feelings and conflicting emotions. We also know that there is extensive evidence about the levels of mental health difficulties faced by many of these young people (Ford *et al* 2007).

These troubled feelings are not likely to go away or even necessarily diminish unless specific help is offered, so it is surely better to plan - and therefore lead - residential care on the basis that it must offer the young people sensitive and engaged support from a team of dedicated staff (Ward 2004). We do of course have to be concerned not to stigmatise or 'pathologise' young people in care, but at the same time we would be doing them a real disservice if we turned a blind eye to their emotional pain (Anglin 2002).

The complication, of course, is that in the everyday context of residential life, the pain and distress is much more likely to be 'enacted' through challenging behaviour and verbal outbursts than to be articulated in the form of direct requests for understanding and support. Additionally, for many of the young people, the causes of the pain are not only in the past but also very much in the present, as they try to cope with the stress of, for example, ongoing conflicts with their parents or other family members. This means that the residential team is likely to be faced with many situations in which young people's understandable distress will 'spill over' into everyday (and every night!) tensions. The advantage of a well-run residential home, however, is that these situations can offer many moments in which skilled workers can seize the chance to offer what I have called 'opportunity-led work' (Ward 2006) - on the spot support, informal counselling and other ways of helping the young people to feel heard, understood and helped. Such work - which often comprises a large proportion of a day's work - requires particular skills and itself needs the support of skilled leadership.

**Example 4.1 Lucy and the evening shift**

The evening shift was drawing towards a close at midnight on a Friday night. The house was relatively quiet, with two of the young people in their rooms with music playing, one in the kitchen making toast and the other three out with friends. The three staff on duty were tired but quite relaxed, and the team leader, Lucy, was writing up notes about an earlier point in the day when Jenny, one of the young people, had received a difficult visit from her mother, who had argued with her daughter about an incident at home a few days previously. Jenny had stormed out of the building, leaving her mother, who herself had eventually left, marooned and angry. Nothing had been resolved, although Jenny had returned soon afterwards (but after her mother had gone) and had retreated to her room. One of the staff, Alice, had sat outside Jenny's room for a while, to let her know she was there to offer support, and had managed to exchange a few words with her, although at this stage Jenny seemed determined to isolate herself.

Late in the evening Alice returned to Jenny's room and found that she was vomiting on the floor after taking an overdose of painkillers. This was out of character for Jenny, and the staff and other young people were very shocked and concerned for her well-being. Alice now took Jenny to the

> emergency department of the local hospital while Lucy supported the other young people and staff together in the kitchen. She was just restoring a sense of calm and understanding when another of the young people returned from her night out, drunk and loud and accompanied by two drunken friends. The night was not over yet …

In this scenario Lucy, the team leader, is effectively holding the place together by remaining in touch and responsive at several levels, communicating with colleagues, containing the anxiety of staff and supporting Alice as well as managing her own internal resources. After all, there may be further difficulties when Jenny and Alice return from the hospital and Lucy will need to pace herself so that she can remain responsive for some time yet. She also knows, however, that if necessary she can telephone the unit leader for informal support and that the next morning she will be able to discuss the night's events with her colleagues and see what can be learned from it.

### Managing the emotional atmosphere of the unit

Because of the high levels of emotion both felt and expressed in the place, a children's home can feel like an environment which can rapidly over-heat, as people 'flare up', sometimes over apparently trivial incidents. A flare-up might take any form, such as a sudden outbreak of verbal abuse between residents or directed at staff, or a fight between residents, or (harder to detect) covert emotional or sexual bullying. Any particular flare-up in itself might not be too disruptive, if it is contained well by the staff, and if nobody is too panicked by it, but if the atmosphere is already volatile, and staff are tired or tense, things can get out of hand very quickly. As we have just seen, a quiet evening can easily be tipped over into a period of escalating difficulty, which will put considerable strain on staff patience, resilience and resourcefulness.

The role of the staff, and especially of the leader, is not only to handle such incidents as they arise, but also to develop a collective ability within the team to read situations and to monitor the atmosphere, so that difficulties can be predicted and where possible prevented, and so that staff can respond positively to any incidents which do arise.

This business of monitoring the atmosphere may involve being aware of subtle changes in the young people's behaviour, such as noticing when excited laughter seems to be turning into something more manic, or alternatively noticing when things seem 'too quiet' in an ominous way. I'm not suggesting that this sort of monitoring of the emotional climate will be carried out in a heavy-handed way, more that an effective staff team and leader tend to develop an instinctive collective awareness of the patterns of daily life and of the possible significance of unexpected changes in these patterns. Part of the leader's educative role with the staff will often be to help newer team members to develop such awareness.

Returning to the metaphor of a potentially-overheating environment, when the leader does notice such a change, an intervention will sometimes be needed which will 'turn down the emotional thermostat' in the place. This might take the form of giving a deliberately calming response to an anxious colleague in order to model the need to lower the emotional temperature. Or it might mean walking quietly through a part of the building in which tension is being expressed through loud or over-excited behaviour, or perhaps engaging more directly with a key individual or sub-group if they seem to be acting as a 'storm-centre' when trouble is brewing. Some such interventions might be taken by the child care staff in their direct work with the young people, while others might be applied to the staff by the leader, to reassure them that collectively they have the capacity and resilience to handle difficult situations. In effect I am suggesting that, in parallel with what is sometimes called the 'chain of command', leadership will also at times involve offering a 'chain of support', bringing positive modelling and a constructive influence which can help to sustain and develop the emotional atmosphere in the place.

It goes without saying that for such work to be clearly within the remit of the leader requires that the leader is sufficiently in contact with the everyday life of the unit to monitor its temperature and to intervene effectively when this is needed. This in turn requires that the leader is close enough to 'ground-level' rather than being (or being perceived to be) too far removed from everyday events in the unit. I emphasize this point because there has sometimes been an argument put forward that leaders in residential homes should concentrate exclusively on their wider responsibilities, such as policy, budgeting and other administrative matters, rather than on the day-to-day care of the young people. By contrast, the whole premise of the 'relationship-based' approach to leadership is that the leader needs to be engaged at all levels, and especially at the level of the daily life of the unit. This means that leadership brings considerable personal demands, of course, as we have seen throughout the discussion, and we shall return to the implications of this for the support and development of leaders in Chapter Seven, 'The Leader as a Person', p.151*ff.*

**Dynamics between leaders and teams**

The discussion has proceeded so far as if leadership was mainly a matter of amicable direction and trusted support - however, we know that this is not always the case. Just as in any other work setting, there may be tensions and unresolved conflicts between teams and their leaders. And despite what I have said about the need for a 'chain of support' there still definitely needs to be a chain of command - which brings into play yet another set of dynamics in the relationships between the leader and the team.

For instance, some members of the team may feel that the leader is either too 'hands-on' and interfering in the detail of their work, or 'hands-off' and uninterested or indifferent to them and their work. In the example above (Example 4.1, pp.84-5), Lucy simply enabled the staff member to take Jenny to the hospital, whereas if she had brusquely ordered her to do so, or perhaps heightened the anxiety and drama by sending for an ambulance which was not really needed, or if she had appeared to allocate an unpopular task to one of the staff and kept an 'easy' option for herself, the whole thing might have turned out very differently. So the leader needs to be conscious of the range of possible ways in which her interventions may be interpreted, and to be able to select the appropriate intervention accordingly. The skill involved in doing so does not come overnight: for example, the leader needs to know him/herself well enough to be able to know the differences between those occasions when a 'tough' intervention is genuinely called for, and when the urge to act in this way may derive more from his or her own insecurity or impatience. When authoritative action *is* needed, the leader needs to be able to feel secure and confident even when others may doubt them or reveal their own insecurities.

Equally the leader may view one member of the team as 'difficult', erratic or unreliable in their work with the young people and may find it hard to offer effective leadership to this person.

**Example 4.2 Erica and the dressing-gown**

In a short-stay children's home a problem developed with a young brother and sister aged 11 and 12 who went through a phase of 'doing a runner' together after bedtime, slipping out of the house and heading off to the bus station in the hope of catching a long-distance bus home to their mother's house.

One night when they were brought back late in the evening by the police, one of the staff, Erica, unhelpfully dramatised the situation further by changing into her night-clothes (she was due to do the sleeping-in duty). As the children arrived in through the front door, escorted by the police officers, Erica appeared in the hall looking worried and unkempt, playing what she intended to be the role of an anxious and sleepless parent - though her appearance puzzled not only the young people but also her colleagues, who possibly saw her rather as Lady Macbeth.

> This bizarre intervention could also have been seen as an undeclared bid for leadership, in that Erica felt that the rest of the team (including the leader) were too accepting or perhaps resigned to this pattern of repeated absconding. She may have been right, of course, but the place to sort out such differences of approach was surely in a staff meeting rather than through amateur dramatics. Needless to say, she was not glad to have this pointed out to her, as she seemed to feel quite proud of her performance!

In this situation the unit leader felt irritated at being distracted from the main task of finding a way of helping these two troubled children to feel more secure in the home, because she had to deal with what felt like the eccentric behaviour of one of the staff. In fact Erica herself was finding the work very distressing and hard to make sense of, especially as she herself was still living nearby in a tense relationship with her own parents. The young people at times became almost protective towards Erica, whose vulnerability they could detect – although when they were feeling more troubled, they could make her life extremely difficult, and she would then retaliate in kind. Eventually Erica moved out of her family home and she also transferred into a more administrative post in which she had no direct contact with troubled young people, and she then began to enjoy her work much more. In the leadership role the manager realised that in order to be able to help those young people more effectively she would have to enable the *whole* unit to work more appropriately and in this case that involved working with Erica towards her move into different work.

## 'Difficult' team members

The scenario involving Erica also reminds us that it is not uncommon in teams for there to be one individual who appears to be the most problematic one to manage. In this case, it seemed clear that Erica herself was finding the work difficult, partly for reasons which were very personal to her, and that this was what was making her 'difficult to manage'. But there are many scenarios in which things may not be so clear-cut, perhaps because other less obvious factors are influencing the dynamics.

For example there may be problematic relationships between various team members, or between one individual and the group as a whole, or even between the team as a whole and some other part of the professional context within which it has to operate. This may involve rivalries or power-struggles, or envy for a team-member who appears to be either the most favoured by the leader, or alternatively perhaps the most popular with the young people. We might all like to think we are 'above such things', but in reality these are all very basic human emotions of the sort which can arise in any work-setting - and especially one as intense as this. Indeed, the fact that most of us prefer to think we are not prone to such feelings ourselves may mean that when we do experience them we may feel so uncomfortable with them that we continue to deny that we have them - even when they are plainly obvious to our colleagues. The feelings will probably then go 'underground', only to emerge in less direct ways. The consequence may be that what the leader has to monitor in the team is the way in which such feelings may be indirectly or covertly affecting people's actions or decisions.

## Workloads and leadership

There are also risks when people are encouraged or allowed to take on too much work. As the next example indicates, they can either exhaust or overstress themselves or unwittingly create other tensions.

### Example 4.3 Doug the rate-buster

In one children's home, Doug, a new and enthusiastic member of staff, would frequently stay on at work after the end of his shift to play football with the children. This made him popular with the children at first, although he soon became less popular with the other staff, as they too came

> under pressure from the children to stay on after work for extra activities. Within a short space of time the new colleague became exhausted, and had to take a week's sick leave, which left everyone else to 'pick up the pieces' and do extra shifts.

The phenomenon in this example is known as 'rate-busting' (that is, when somebody exceeds or 'busts' the team's work rate). Although this term originated in factory work, it is surprising how often the same pattern also emerges in other settings. In this example, it was not clear at first whether Doug was trying to court popularity with the young people or trying to impress the manager by always 'going the extra mile' even when that extra mile was not necessary! He was inexperienced and genuinely surprised at how things turned out, and further discussion revealed that he had chosen this field of work partly because he wanted a ready-made group of younger siblings who would be grateful for his indulgent extra games with them. Leaders need to monitor and discourage this sort of work-pattern, while also taking care that they do not themselves provide a model of someone who works excessive hours, giving the impression to other team members that this is what is expected.

In situations such as this, the leader's skill will lie in seeing beyond the immediate 'problem person' and identifying the other possible factors - in other words, taking a 'whole-system' approach and considering the apparent problem as maybe just one symptom of a whole set of interactions and relationships. Where a major difficulty appears to be developing, therefore, the leader has to try to discover what exactly is going on, and why it is happening, before deciding how to intervene to improve the situation.

Handling such situations may be quite hard for managers, especially as it is not uncommon for people's difficulties to be expressed through direct conflict with the leader. A person who is angry about the sort or amount of work required may see this as the sole responsibility of the team leader. How can the leader then switch roles from being seen as the 'bad' person who has imposed something on the individual that they cannot or will not handle, to being a 'good' person who can help the worker to sort out the difficulty?

The leader may feel drawn into either 'putting their foot down' and insisting that the work must be done or perhaps into 'rescuing' the person (and the situation) by backing down and reallocating work elsewhere. At different times either of these responses can be appropriate but it may be that neither is of help. When one person is expressing difficulties on behalf of the team as a whole, what is needed most is an honest and open debate between the leader and the team about issues such as the stresses of the work and the availability of support. However, in order to open up this sort of debate, the leader may need the support of an external trainer or group facilitator, who can 'hold the ropes' between the leader and the team or individual. This need not involve the leader losing face, in fact it can enable all sides to feel listened to and regain their morale and engagement with the team as a whole (Obholzer and Roberts 1994).

**Working at ground level: opportunity led leadership.** Leadership, as we have seen in many of the examples given so far, involves more than just the formal business such as the chairing of meetings or the drawing up of policies. Much of it happens at 'ground level' in the everyday interactions in the unit, in encounters with individuals and groups of young people, or working alongside other staff who are engaged with the young people. It is important that the leader spends sufficient time working at ground level, and often doing so in a quiet or unassuming way. It may not be necessary for the leader to be especially demonstrative in their style: everyone is likely to be aware of their role and their authority, and very often it may be better to underplay the role rather than over-play it.

For example, being willing to spend time alongside junior staff in humdrum tasks, or relaxing with colleagues over coffee at the end of a shift, may be just as useful in building the relationship between leader and team as any of the more formal tasks. The concept of '*management by walking about*' (*cf* Huczynski 1993) became popular in the 1990s and was sometimes parodied with implications that 'walking about' was all that managers ever did or needed to do, but we have already seen that in the residential setting there is real value in the leader being seen as involved and engaged at various levels, and thus seen as concerned not just with the task but with the people doing the task. Again this may become clearer if we picture a leader who is *never* seen at ground level and who is then likely to be experienced as remote and uncaring.

Another aspect of valuing the everyday work of leadership is that, just as in practice much of the most effective work with young people happens in the unplanned in-between moments when an opportunity may arise for useful communication (Ward 2006), so the same will often happen in the leader's work with the team. The task of the leader will be to spot the opportunity and find an appropriate way to respond.

**Example 4.4 Grace and the office door**

Grace was the head of a hostel or 'foyer' for homeless youth in a provincial city. She had become concerned at the way in which some staff appeared to be distancing themselves from the young people, frequently retreating to the office when on duty and even shutting the door so that they seemed quite unavailable to the young people. Staff justified this position on the grounds that they had so much paperwork to do and that in any case the young people 'had to learn to be independent', but to Grace this all seemed to have been taken too far.

One day as she walked past the office door Grace saw Carina, one of the young people, standing outside by the door looking nervous. Grace began talking with Carina, and after a few minutes she quietly opened the office door and led Carina in by the hand, sat down with her and held a conversation with her, gradually drawing in the other staff and involving them in the conversation which became more relaxed and even animated. As another young person came to the door Grace beckoned to him to come in, too. Later in the day at the handover meeting one of the staff expressed annoyance that Grace had brought the young people into the office, but Grace steered this discussion into a debate about the young people's genuine need for advice, acceptance and befriending, even while they also needed to move gradually towards greater emotional independence. In the long run the office returned to its 'staff only' status, but the staff began to emerge and engage with the young people much more frequently.

In this example Grace took advantage - in an unplanned way - of the moment which had presented itself, by simply doing what she would have liked the staff to do, even though she risked causing some confusion and irritation by breaking their conventions. It paid off in the long run as staff began to recognise that having more contact with the young people was not only valued by the young people, but also brought more satisfaction and fulfilment for the staff themselves, as they became more confident in their own ability to offer real support and advice.

If leaders are to take advantage of the opportunities for useful communication which arise informally in everyday work, they need to become adept not only at monitoring what is happening in the place, but also at spotting and using the opportunities when they arise: these skills are very similar to those needed for opportunity led work with young people.

Sometimes what arises is the opportunity not just for a leadership intervention but also for a 'training and development' one, as Collie has described (2002). There are also many good opportunities for 'live' or 'real-time' supervision:

**Example 4.5 Selina and 'live' supervision**

Ahmed had spent the last forty minutes trying to contain Tom, a young boy who had flown into a rage with another boy and had had to be removed

> to his own room so that he could not harm others. Tom was no longer being physically violent but he was still very angry, and Ahmed was trying to get through the rage and was beginning to help Tom to recognise what was really troubling him, which seemed to stem from his feeling of rejection by his mother after a recent weekend at home that had gone badly wrong.
>
> The unit manager, Selina, sat on the floor outside Tom's bedroom, with the door slightly ajar so that both Ahmed and Tom knew she was there, but not directly intervening. Occasionally either Tom or Ahmed would call out to her or ask her a question, and at one point she brought in a coffee and biscuit for each of them. She could tell that this was turning into an important time for Tom to unburden himself through talking with Ahmed, but equally she was aware of the strain on Ahmed, who was drained after several days on shift without a proper break. After the situation was eventually brought to an end, Selina was in a good position to help Ahmed de-brief and learn from the whole incident. It was also important to Tom that Ahmed had been able to stay with him throughout his anger and distress.

Of course, support of this sort can be offered between any two colleagues on shift together, but it is especially valuable if the unit leader is also sometimes involved at this level - partly so that she remains in close contact with the current concerns of the young people but also so that she can use this medium to reinforce whatever models of everyday work she is promoting, though modelling. For example, Selina may have wished to promote the use of this sort of 'live supervision' as a means of mutual support within the team, and on this occasion she was able to demonstrate its value both to staff and to young people.

**Summary**

This chapter has focused on the relationship between the leader and the team, especially with regard to helping the team to handle their emotional task with the young people. We have looked not only at the overall relationship between leader and team, but also at the ideas of 'ground-level' work and 'opportunity-led leadership'. What has also emerged from the discussion is the real importance, in a relationship-based approach, of the leader being sufficiently in touch with the everyday life and concerns both of the team and of the young people themselves. In the next chapter we will add to all this a discussion of what goes on beneath the surface of leadership, in the unconscious interactions between leaders and teams.

CHAPTER FIVE

# Below the surface: unconscious dynamics

This chapter covers the *un*conscious dynamics of leadership - the things which go on below the surface between leaders and others but which may nevertheless have a major impact on how leadership (and therefore the whole organisation) operates. The chapter describes and explains some of these phenomena and shows how some of the key concepts can help leaders to understand their role and achieve the more difficult aspects of their task. In doing so it introduces a number of main ideas from the literature that approaches organisations from a psychodynamic and systems perspective (NB A good place to start in that literature is *The Unconscious at Work* by Obholzer & Roberts, 1997).

I am well aware that some people feel that psychoanalytic ideas belong more properly (if at all) in the consulting room or clinic rather than in discussing team behaviour and leadership matters, while others find aspects of this whole approach difficult or perhaps not really relevant. However, my own view is that this is just another way of trying to make sense of some of the more puzzling and problematic aspects of leadership and of organisational life in general - one which offers some useful insights into what may sometimes (though not always) be happening below the surface to influence current behaviour. So when trying to unravel difficult issues in the work, although I would always want to start with the more 'practical' and rational approaches, I would say that there also times when more psychological theories can be especially helpful.

## The unconscious

The discussion in the previous chapters has mostly proceeded as if the relationships between leaders, teams and young people are always conducted and experienced at a purely rational level, involving straightforward discussion, decision-making and direct communication. If this were really the case, however, then life would be a lot simpler than it often turns out to be in the real world - where people do behave ‘oddly’, irrationally or unpredictably, and where they frequently misread each other's intentions and over-react to particular personality types or to certain kinds of issue. In fact there are all sorts of things going on below the surface between leaders and teams in every organisation, and residential homes are no exception. Sometimes, for example, crises may seem to explode out of nowhere, and people may get unreasonably upset or troubled, or get under each other's skin, sometimes setting off surprisingly strong reactions all round. As a leader it can be very frustrating to be trying to grapple with behaviour and events that feel unpredictable, inexplicable or beyond your influence, and it is in these situations that the psychodynamic approach can help to explain and interpret what is going on.

**Projection, transference and counter-transference**

One way in which the unconscious may be at work is through the mechanism of projection. Projection is where we might attribute to another person some particular set of feelings which we *imagine* they may be feeling, although in reality these may be turn out to be our own feelings which we are 'reading' onto them. Because all of this is happening at an unconscious level we are not usually aware of it, and yet it may play a very significant part in our working relationships.

The literature suggests that there are some very powerful templates half-hidden in the background in most people's relationships with leaders - these may be models either of parental or of other key relationships. Thus for example we may perhaps instinctively rebel against a leader who reminds us of our father or feel protective to one who reminds us of our mother - or *vice versa*, depending on our own earlier relationship with our parents. We may not be very conscious of the ways in which we are reminded of these parental relationships, but that doesn't mean the influence is not there. This is one reason why the dynamics of leadership may become so complicated and confusing, because we each tend to unwittingly bring our own constellation of prior relationships to bear upon our current networks, and then interpret people's words and behaviour in line with these templates, and react to them accordingly - sometime setting off further reactions.

**Example 5.1 David, Annette and 'Mumsy'**

David, a residential manager, spoke warmly with his colleague Annette about Gloria, a senior manager whom he had found particularly supportive and enabling - only to find that Annette dismissed Gloria angrily as 'Mumsy' (by which she meant 'patronising and sentimental'). From Annette's point of view, having a leader with a stereotypical 'maternal' persona was always going to lead to trouble, whereas for David it was fine. They were each reacting to the same person in very different ways.

These dynamics may operate in both directions, though, and in this case it seemed that the manager, Gloria, perceived each of these colleagues in turn as if David was a dutiful son and Annette a rebellious daughter and she treated them accordingly - but if this was indeed so, was she really able to be an effective leader? In many ways Gloria was quite effective, although she was perhaps not fully in control of the 'messages' she was giving out. Maybe she had her own reasons (from her own background) to play up her persona as a nurturing maternal figure, and had found this effective in some previous work situations, but on the other hand perhaps she was not able to modify this persona in those contexts (or with those individuals) where it was less helpful.

It so happened that there seemed to be a good 'fit' between Gloria and David in that they responded to each other in largely positive terms. But things were much less positive between her and Annette, who was nevertheless an extremely effective worker herself, even though she sometimes felt patronised and alienated by her manager. Meanwhile, just to complicate things further, there was another female senior manager in the same organisation who was

> much more 'pushy' and demanding, and whom David found much more difficult to cope with, but whom Annette probably found much easier!

It is this sort of situation in which a purely rational approach may not be very helpful, if it leads to such conflicts being seen as down to one party or another 'just being difficult', or simply due to a 'personality clash' - and therefore, in some people's view, as just one of those things which can't be helped or put right. In this context when I hear the term 'personality clash' I often feel that people are retreating into a blind alley and imagining that nothing can change. A more psychologically-based approach to this situation might enable people to understand both their own and each other's feelings rather better and hopefully then to modify their behaviour so that the potential for damaging conflict could be reduced.

Projection is one aspect of the processes of *transference* and *counter-transference* in relationships. These terms refer to the set of assumptions which we all unwittingly bring to our interactions with other people - and in the present context, especially to the feelings which leaders and team members may bring to their interactions with each other, perhaps experiencing one person as more irritating or attractive than another, as a result of their own personal history. Transference refers to the way in which we may unwittingly 'transfer' our feelings about key figures in our personal past on to the actual individuals we encounter in everyday life - responding to our manager as if they were our parent, for instance, or to a junior colleague as if they were a rebellious adolescent, as we saw in the example above. Naturally most of us are reluctant to think that we are driven by factors such as this, as we prefer to feel that we ourselves are rational and clear-thinking - so it's usually easier to see these influences at work in other people than in oneself.

*Counter*-transference, meanwhile, refers to the reciprocal process by which the leader may either react (unconsciously) to the other person's transference - treating a challenging team member as a tiresome child, for example - or in which the leader may bring her own unwitting assumptions into the frame, perhaps treating *all* team members as if they were children. This is the sort of thing we saw in Gloria's respective treatment of Dave and Annette in the earlier example. When one person's template sparks off another's in a 'perfect fit' things can get very lively, and not usually for the better.

The templates which we each bring to bear in these situations are not all the same, of course, and they do not all relate to parent-child relationships, but sometimes to the competitive feelings between siblings, or perhaps to the attractions between flirting lovers, or to the anxieties about separation and loss which seem to permeate some relationships, to choose just a few powerful examples. In our personal lives we will all have experienced some version of most of these powerful feelings.

At a rational level there may seem to be no logical reason why unconscious feelings such as those I have been describing should seep into the supposedly less intense world of work-relationships. And yet the reality is that they often do, especially in residential child care where the focus on relationships is one of the main tools of everyday practice. This is also a setting in which work-relationships themselves can be very intense, long-lasting and significant in many ways and may develop something of the flavour of close personal relationships. Psychodynamic theory suggests that where particular types of relationship in our personal experience have been left unresolved, or where we have retained especially strong feelings around a certain theme, these feelings may continue to replay in our minds. It also suggests that we may even unconsciously seek to re-enact the relationships in order to try to resolve those feelings. Thus we will find scenarios and settings to 'play out' these unresolved parts of ourselves, and this can happen at work just as much as it does outside of work.

This might all start to sound rather remote from the practical demands of leadership, especially as so much of it may be going on at an unconscious level of which neither side is fully aware. And yet it often turns out to underpin some of the more intractable problems which can arise for leaders, because if unrecognized it may (for example) contribute to a leader unconsciously withholding key information from a staff member who has 'got under her skin' in a negative way or perhaps to her unwittingly 'turning a blind eye' to inappropriate behaviour on the part of another worker whom she may unconsciously favour or tolerate inappropriately. We saw an example of this in Chapter Three in the case of Anne and the 'too-chummy' team leader, Mike (Example 3.5, pp.74-5). In situations such as this, the leader's judgement and actions may become distorted in ways that could have serious consequences for the quality of the service offered. This is why these seemingly intractable problems in the relationship between the leader and team members really matter - because if left unaddressed they may seriously affect the quality of the service that is offered to the young people.

**Projective identification**

Another way in which unconscious feelings may affect our work as leaders is through projective identification: this refers to the way in which we may unconsciously 'pick up' *other* people's powerful feelings and experience them as if they were our own feelings. This may happen because the person with whom the feelings originated found them too hard to handle him- or herself, and perhaps denied the feelings, although still somehow (and probably unconsciously) managing to convey them to us 'under our radar', with the result that we may end up experiencing the feelings *for* them. The consequence is that we may find we are left experiencing unaccountably strong feelings, which can even sometimes be felt bodily as well as emotionally, and the origins of which we cannot easily trace even though they still feel very powerful - and which may then affect or distort our judgement.

**Example 5.2 Mary arrives home**

Mary was driving home after a day's work as leader of a children's home. It had been a demanding day as usual, mostly spent in supervising new staff, but she felt satisfied with her input and was looking forward to a simple relaxing evening.

But as she arrived home and opened her front door, Mary noticed that her hand was shaking, as if with fear or anger. She realised that she was feeling quite tense, but was not sure why this should be so, and as she went into the house and sat down she found that she was beginning to shake more and more powerfully. Her mind was also agitated, and she found herself tracking back through the day's work, as if searching for an explanation of her state of mind. She couldn't identify anything in particular, but she found herself replaying in her mind a moment in her supervision of Josie, one of her newer and younger staff.

Josie had briefly mentioned (in a flat tone of voice) an incident the night before when a young person, Sharon, had described sometimes feeling at risk physically when at home with her father. As Josie had been talking with Mary in supervision, she had appeared to be out of her depth in that piece of work, and she had passed quickly over the details of her conversation with Sharon without really registering her concern for the young person's welfare.

What Mary now realized was that she, too, had under-played her own response and had neither really recognized Sharon's own fear nor helped Josie with learning how to handle such strong feelings. It was only now as she reached home that Mary began to recognize what her agitated body and troubled mind had been telling her: that she was now experiencing the fear for Sharon's welfare that Josie was too anxious to recognize in herself, as well as Sharon's own fear. Josie had unwittingly conveyed her anxiety, despite her lifeless account of the conversation, and in turn Mary had 'picked it up' without realising, only for it to re-emerge as soon as the other pressures of the day were off.

In this scenario, which was later relayed to me in a staff consultation meeting, Mary was experienced enough to recognize that if something did not feel right, there was probably a good reason for this. Very often realisations such as these come about because we find ourselves left with a feeling which we cannot really explain, or whose intensity doesn't appear to fit with the circumstances. The clue which Mary had noticed in passing but had not initially acted on was the odd flatness of Josie's account of the conversation with Sharon, a flatness that contrasted with the drama hinted at in the content. It was only much later in the day when she noticed her own physical symptom of her shaking hand that she began to realise that something was not right. In fact that very flatness had been a hint in itself, a communication in its own right, but one whose meaning needed to be unlocked by making some connections.

To make sense of a situation in which projective identification has played a role we may then need to ask ourselves questions such as:

- Where does this strength of feeling come from?

or as Robin Shohet put it, in an excellent chapter on this subject (Shohet 1999),

- "Whose feelings am I feeling?"

If we can use this sort of question to help us unravel such puzzling phenomena, we may find that the idea of projective identification can help us to make sense of some of the most difficult situations and work out appropriate responses to them. In order to do so, leaders need an ability to develop their own reflective mind, to ask themselves key questions as if they could be their own internal supervisor (Casement 1990), as well as using an *external* supervisor or consultant to help them explore their own emotional / psychological state.

**Working with the unconscious**

So what is the answer to dealing with forces which may be operating unconsciously like this? The responsibility of the leader is to aim to become sufficiently insightful and self-aware to be more mindful of these sorts of dynamics, and to promote a working culture in which it is OK to acknowledge their existence. The problem is that what is unconscious generally tends to *remain* unconscious, although it does often manage to find expression through indirect means, which may then offer us hints and clues if we are able to tune in to them - as in the case of the flat tone of voice in the example above. So with sufficient help and insight we can learn to be more aware of the effects of the unconscious, hopefully tracing it back to its roots, and managing it better within ourselves.

In the earlier case of David and his feelings about different female managers, for example, he had to learn to acknowledge his mixed feelings about his expressive and affectionate mother and his more remote and inhibited father, and about the lingering legacy left by these relationships. Only then could he begin to work out how these dynamics might be affecting both his leadership style and his ability or otherwise to work alongside colleagues and superiors. David made the decision to get some help in understanding himself through psychotherapy, and this was of great benefit to him in this respect, as it helped him learn how to distinguish between his own 'issues' and other people's behaviour and expectations. While not everyone will want to look to psychotherapy for such support, it can undoubtedly be helpful to have some experience of psychodynamic thinking and of applying it to one's own understanding of self-in-relationship before trying to use it to explain *other* people's behaviour and relationships.

**Re-enactment**

In the residential child care context, unconscious dynamics such as those we have been exploring may have a particular power to them because - as we have seen - there are already likely to be some very strong feelings flying around amongst the young people about their own relationships with their parents and other key figures. In addition there are often strong feelings present in the staff, not only about these particular children and their families, but also (and less consciously) about their own families of origin. Some people, for example, may feel quite angry and even punitive towards parents who might be seen as having 'failed' their children. Because feelings such as these may feel as if they are unacceptable, they may be denied and not consciously known about, although they will be none the less real, and they may find indirect expression instead, as people unconsciously enact the feelings in their interactions with the parents or in decision-making meetings.

The concept of re-enactment is particularly helpful as it suggests that 'that which we fail to understand we in some manner enact' (Danbury and Wallbridge 1989). In other words, if we experience distress, anxiety or panic which is not easy to make sense of or even to acknowledge, perhaps because it relates to uncomfortable material such as parental conflict, then sometimes these feelings are likely to remain underground. Such feelings will then be held on to but not expressed, because they feel too threatening, powerful or shameful. And yet they may nevertheless find expression through other means, perhaps through re-playing them in similar situations such as those that arise in daily life in residential care. This concept of re-enactment helps to explain how the unresolved or unmanaged conflict in one group (e.g. adolescents in a care home) may get replayed among another parallel group (the staff team), leading to 'acting out' in which team members may unwittingly take on the role or behaviour of certain adolescents. This is sometimes also known as 'parallel process' (Miller, S, 2004):

**Example 5.3 Patrick and Miriam re-enacting**

A furious row suddenly broke out one day between Patrick and Miriam, who were both staff members in a home for adolescents. The argument was triggered by a minor incident in which the kitchen had been left in an untidy state by Patrick. These workers were normally good friends and colleagues, and both were surprised and hurt by the intensity of their argument. Subsequent discussion in a staff meeting revealed that they had both been troubled by another uncomfortable and unexplained argument a few days before, this time between a male and a female resident whom they had been working with. On that occasion there had been verbal threats of violence and retaliation on both sides between these young people - and again this had been in the context of a previously close friendship.

As this story unfolded in a supervision group, it became clear that although the staff had been aware of the argument between the residents, they had not intervened or even commented, because of other anxieties, which meant that the strong feelings had been left hanging in the air. Patrick and Miriam were each privately troubled by this

> tension but had not felt able to share these feelings with each other in a 'professional' way, and had ended up unconsciously replaying the conflict because they were both still anxious and puzzled. Once the parallel between their own behaviour and that of the young people was recognised, their own friendship soon over-rode the tension and they realised that they now needed to go back to the young people and address the earlier conflict and especially the threats of violence.

In this situation it was relatively easy to identify the components in the parallel process, but it is not always so straightforward. When there is an outbreak of unexplained feelings or actions, it is always worth searching around in the emotional 'undergrowth' of the unit to find parallels, because these will usually emerge sooner or later. In order to unravel and make sense of situations and feelings such as these it can be very helpful for the staff team (including the leader) to participate in a regular group meeting - perhaps led by an outside adviser - to focus on the feelings within the staff team and between team members and others. In the example just given, once the original conflict between the two young people had been addressed and resolved (as far as it could be), the tension went out of the whole unit ... until the next incident. It is also worth noting here that, although the argument between

Patrick and Miriam seemed unpleasant and even unprofessional at the time, it served a useful function in the long run by enabling them to return eventually to their half-submerged concern about the earlier tension between the young people, which was otherwise likely to continue festering in the unit and probably affecting others' behaviour too.

So processes such as projective identification, uncomfortable though they may be to face, can often be used and in a sense harnessed towards the overall task of the care of the young people. The key is to work at understanding the process, and one important role of leadership is therefore to watch for unconscious dynamics such as these, and to find ways of addressing them where they do arise and helping people to acknowledge such factors - and as far as possible to avoid getting drawn into these dynamics in the first place, though that is much harder!

**Unconscious motivations**

If we look at people's motivation for deciding to work in child care - and especially for *staying* in it - there are often connections with aspects of their own childhood and specifically with their own early experience of feeling 'looked after' or otherwise. They may have quite strong feelings about all of this, some of them unconscious, driving a need to (for example) seek to repair their own difficult childhood by providing a better one for others, or more complicatedly, trying to indirectly punish their own 'bad' parents by removing or 'rescuing' other children from their supposedly bad parents. In fact, if we are honest, most of us can find some trace of these sorts of feelings lurking within us, and it is probably better to acknowledge and address them where possible rather than to be unwittingly driven by them. Some of these motivations may appear problematic and unworthy, while others are not so inappropriate so long as we are aware of them and in control of them.

These unconscious motivations in staff may affect the leadership role too, because leaders have to tolerate and work with all sorts of feelings projected onto them by both staff and children. In any organisation leaders may find themselves seen as fathers or mothers or as older brothers, as remote authority figures, threatening siblings or even as 'perfect' idols, and in residential child care all the more so. To some extent they just have to experience and live with these feelings and not feel too threatened or uncomfortable with them. The greater challenge will arise when there is either a particularly strong 'match' or clash between the expectations on each side.

**Example 5.4 Paul the over-identified leader**

Paul was the leader of a small unit working with young people at risk of homelessness and substance abuse. His own history as a teenager had included being temporarily thrown out of his family home at 16 when his mother took a new partner, although there had later been a reconciliation. His colleagues, of course, knew nothing of this personal background, but when he talked in supervision it soon became clear that when at work he would often have his own troubled adolescence in the back of his mind.

It seemed to be on the basis of this history that Paul felt such a powerful identification with some of the young people in the unit, and at times it was as if he wanted to fight all their battles for them. He would often take their side unquestioningly in their conflicts with parents and authorities, sometimes in a counter-productive way that would ultimately leave him emotionally exhausted, so that (ironically) he was then much less able to help the young people than he had hoped.

With the help of his supervisor, however, Paul gradually learned to understand and manage his own powerful feelings, and to channel them into supporting the team in running an excellent facility rather than trying to take on everything and everyone himself. They still didn't know - and didn't need to know - about his personal history, but because he now understood it better himself it affected the quality of his work less.

## Containment and holding

Much of the work that leaders have to do with their teams in the residential child care context is about working with anxiety. This includes the anxiety which staff may feel in relation to their work with the young people, the anxiety which the young people and their families experience in their lives through whatever difficulties have brought them to the place, as well as the anxiety of others about the place and how it works.

When we acknowledge that leadership in this setting is stressful we are likely to be thinking of these sorts of anxiety, and of how the leader may feel he or she has to 'soak it all up' in order to keep the place running. In fact this 'soaking up' metaphor is not a very healthy one, because it suggests that the leader has to simply keep on absorbing more and more of the anxiety - which would not be good for anyone. Equally, though, it would not be helpful for the leader to ignore the anxiety and try to place him- or herself at a distance from it, perhaps by denying it and constantly either jollying people along, or simply giving mechanical orders and only dealing with the practical elements in the job. Both staff members and the young people themselves want to feel listened to and understood - and if they don't feel understood they are likely to express their feelings in more and more dramatic (though sometimes indirect) ways, as we have seen.

So if leaders should neither absorb all the anxiety nor deny or ignore it, what *should* they do with it? The metaphors used in the psychodynamic approach are those of 'holding' and 'containment', and these both originate in slightly different interpretations of the experience of babies and young children, especially their experience of the natural cycles of upset, distress and feeling comforted. In the view of Wilfred Bion (1962), the parent (usually - though not necessarily - the mother) responds to the child's natural distress and anxiety by 'containing' it: being willing to experience the fears and terrors of insecurity on behalf of the child by temporarily 'looking after' these strong feelings and then gradually handing them back to the child in a more manageable form, so that the baby feels 'contained'.

If we now translate this scenario into its equivalent in the professional setting, the template which it offers is of the leader as a parental figure 'containing' the anxiety which he or she picks up in the place - but not to just soak it up and hold on to it, rather to think about it, acknowledge and reflect it back to people in manageable forms.

**Example 5.5 Jackie containing the wild 'Peter'**

Jackie was the manager of an 'ordinary' children's home for a mixture of young people, some of whom had lived there for several years. After a very settled period with few changes, two of the long-standing residents left and within a short space two new much younger children (a brother and sister of 12 and 10 respectively) were admitted. The house rapidly became chaotic as the boy in particular - Peter - ran a personal riot around the place, often becoming wildly angry and sometimes breaking things and lashing out at people. The situation deteriorated as the rest of the young people, and some of the staff, became resentful at the level of disruption and at what seemed like the real risk that someone would get hurt. It began to seem that Peter was 'unreachable'. Some staff were very angry with him, some felt protective towards him and critical of their angry colleagues, while the general level of anxiety in the place escalated rapidly.

In her leadership role, Jackie had to work closely with the staff team to enable them to 'contain' both Peter himself (by allocating him a key worker and back-up who between them would focus closely on meeting his everyday needs and feelings) and the rest of the group (by reassuring and calming them, and letting them know that Peter was now starting to feel better). As Peter began to feel less anxious himself, everyone else's anxiety levels also began to drop.

This sort of containment will often involve a great deal of listening and seeking to understand, as well as sometimes a steely determination to persevere with genuine containment rather than giving up, despairing and then having to resort to the apparently easier but actually far less productive option of punishment. In this case the team was also able to use the regular 'house meetings' between staff and young people not only to allow the frustrations on all sides to be expressed but also to promote some understanding within the whole group about Peter's needs, reminding the other young people of their own fears and anxieties when they had first arrived. Eventually the larger group could play a part in enabling Peter to feel safer and more accepted.

As this example shows, the sense of containment does not all need to be provided personally by the leader, and indeed it *should* not - that would be to centre and focus too much dependency on a single figure. A well-functioning management system will mean that most of the distress and anxiety of the young people will be contained by the staff in most daily contact with them, while much of the anxiety of those staff will in turn be contained by their supervisors and team leaders, with the unit manager providing an overall sense of the whole thing being contained. Perhaps a helpful image here would be of the Russian dolls which are 'nested' one inside another.

The other key concept here is of the 'holding environment': this term comes from Winnicott's account

(1965) of the same process of infant care. He interprets the anxieties of a baby as relating to fears such as falling apart, falling forever, etc. He writes of the parent(s) providing for the child a 'holding environment' by which he means a secure sense of being understood, wanted and loved, and of behaviour and emotion being tolerable and meaningful; this is provided by a combination of physical and emotional responsiveness.

This again is a useful metaphor for the way in which a leader can provide an overall 'holding environment' for the young people by ensuring that the emotional climate of the place remains accepting, giving and positive, despite the challenges and difficulties which the young people may present. As we have just seen, a true holding environment will also include the supporting role that the young people may be able to provide for each other.

This will mean providing an environment and relationships that meet the emotional stage of the young person as well as their chronological age. It will mean an environment that is subtly and flexibly adapted for each young person while also offering enough overall consistency. This challenges the grown-ups to be creative to meet needs rather than challenge the young people to conform to what is being provided as a 'programme'. Incidentally, Laura Steckley has also written very usefully (2012) about how the sort of emotional 'holding environment' which has been discussed here can help to prevent the need for much of the physical restraint which is otherwise often needed in residential care when young people's behaviour becomes risky and unmanageable.

### Summary

This chapter has offered an introduction to some key concepts in the psychodynamic approach to leadership and applied them to the residential child care context. The message is that what happens below the surface may sometimes turn out to be at least as important as the more pragmatic approaches in helping us to make sense of some of the powerful and challenging situations in this work. I am not advocating that this is the only approach to draw upon, nor that it will always provide the right answer, but that when taken with the other approaches in this book, it can add significantly to our understanding.

CHAPTER SIX

# Leadership in the Context of Values: Power, Prejudice and Dependency.

In this chapter we focus on the question of personal and professional values and on the powerful ways in which these values can underpin some of the dilemmas which arise in everyday practice, especially in the relationships between the leader, the team and the young people.

## The Values of Leadership

Leadership is discussed by some as if it was a mechanical science, in which - so long as the necessary components are put in place and the right connections properly wired up - everything will run like clockwork. Others meanwhile describe it as if it were one of the arts, requiring personal qualities and inventiveness, including skill in 'conducting' the whole ensemble of the organisation as if it was an orchestra, and I confess to leaning in this direction. A more balanced view would perhaps incorporate both of these elements - the technical and the expressive - although there would still be something vital missing if the leadership role was not underpinned by a clear set of values.

In all forms of social care there needs to be an underlying awareness of the values inherent in the work. The beliefs and moral positions which have been held in mind (at least implicitly) in the planning and delivery of the service must then find expression at every level, and in every detail of the way the service is delivered. These values are often underpinned by formal statements such as official Codes of Ethics, in addition to the legal frameworks that apply, so they are in no sense optional or incidental - they need to be built into the foundations of the whole enterprise.

There is therefore a particular responsibility on leaders to embody and promote the values of the service: if the leader doesn't actively and visibly promote these values it will be much harder for anyone else to do so with much effectiveness, or for the leader to expect others to do so. Among the values that we might include would be:

- A fundamental respect for other people at all levels, whatever their role may be as either offering or receiving care;

- A commitment to respect people's privacy and to preserve confidentiality;

- An active concern to promote the safety and well-being of the residents and to harness the work of the place to support this aim;

- A commitment to promoting an approach based on understanding, tolerance and inclusiveness;

- An active commitment to valuing difference and diversity and to redressing inequality;

- A willingness to listen to and incorporate others' views, within the working methods and the organisational culture of the place.

Since so much does centre upon the leader's way of working, it is fair to assume that his or her actions and statements will be continually 'read' for the message which they convey about how people should treat each other. Leaders therefore have to not only speak clearly about values but also embody them in their actions and aim to model values-led practice. In fact whether or not they aim to do so, their actions will still be scrutinized and people will 'take their lead' from the leader, justifying themselves on the basis of how they interpret what they see. This means that leadership itself is a moral activity, in which aiming to practise as you preach is essential.

Within this framework of values I want to use the rest of this chapter to develop the themes of power, prejudice and dependency, which I have argued elsewhere (Ward 2006) to be central to all group care practice, and which is certainly true of leadership in the residential child care context. Of course, all leaders operate within a context of the dynamics of power and dependency, and have to address issues of prejudice at many levels. In addition these matters arise and interact critically in the lives of the young people being cared for, and therefore are bound to affect the ways in which all relationships between young people, staff and leaders operate.

### Power

We may think we know what we mean by the term 'power', but it is not always as logical or straightforward as we might imagine. For example, even though all leadership does involve the use of power and authority, and leaders are often perceived as powerful people, they may not always feel very powerful themselves, and they may feel constrained as to what they can actually do to remedy or 'solve' difficult situations. For one thing, organisational rules and policies will sometimes mean there is little scope for creative responses from the leader, but there may also be very personal factors involved, such as the leader's own level of confidence and authority. In other words, power can be a subjective as well as an objective quality.

In care homes, leaders may use their power to seek to influence and even inspire people: to encourage staff to try new ways of working, for instance, or to help residents to believe that they themselves may have more to offer than they realize. At other times the leader may need to act powerfully to restore a sense of well-being in a troubled group of young people, or to challenge a staff member or a whole team about some aspect of their practice. Leadership may also involve protecting the unit from criticism or suspicion coming from outside, whether from neighbours or perhaps from other professionals, and this protection may require the leader to be assertive and directive. The leader will also have to represent the unit and its work at external meetings. In all of these scenarios the leader is exercising power that relies on a combination of personal and organisational authority. Discussion in previous chapters has highlighted the process of establishing personal authority, but we also have to be mindful of the extent to which the larger organisation both sanctions and supports the leader's own judicious use of power and authority.

An important additional factor here is that the issue of power is central to the experience of children and young people in residential care, especially because they will have very often been on the receiving end of other people's exercise of power, sometimes including others' abuse of such power. They may have been attacked, ignored or abused in their own homes, excluded from their schools and other societal institutions, and they may often have been moved from one place to another with little consultation or warning. Relationships which may at first have seemed promising, such as those with foster carers, may have broken down suddenly and irretrievably, while others such as teachers and social workers may have lost patience with them and effectively rejected them.

Experiences such as these may leave the young people with confused, uncertain or distorted expectations of adults, and especially of adults in power such as care staff and managers, and as we know they may then express these feelings of powerlessness and frustration by taking them out on the staff and especially on the leader. We know also that troubled adolescents in particular may themselves be perceived as powerful because they can act in threatening or aggressive ways, although the reality is that it is often they who are terrified within, even if they can't easily admit this to anyone, least of all to themselves. They may also find it very difficult to trust or respect what the leader of the home may say, because they have so often felt let down and rejected by those in power, and so they may react in such a way as to make the leader, too, feel quite criticised, devalued and rejected.

All of this means that leaders have to operate with great sensitivity to the ways in which their own use of power may be perceived. It will of course be essential at times to be very firm and assertive in setting down rules and expectations, but if that is *all* that leaders do, they are unlikely to gain much respect or to bring about much change in the young people, even though they might enforce a superficial compliance. Power therefore needs to be thought about and negotiated within the context of the relationships involved, and the first responsibility of the leader is to work at promoting the best quality of relationships between all concerned: this is part of what is meant by a 'relationship-based' approach. With young people in care this will mean painstaking work not only with each individual but also with the group as a whole, to create a climate in which people will be able to safely express their thoughts and feelings to and about each other. This often means working to restore young people's own sense of dignity by treating them with respect and genuine care, and seeking to redress the sense of stigma from which many of them may suffer.

All of this is much easier said than done, and in a place where trust and dignity have broken down or have perhaps become diminished they can take many months of hard work to re-establish. Once this does start to happen, however, the benefits for the young people can be enormous in terms of their increased confidence and ability to relate positively with each other and with those seeking to support and help them.

One effective way of working towards the establishment of trust and openness will be to hold regular group meetings for all staff and residents at which there is an open agenda for everyone to raise and debate any matters which are of importance to them – in other words, to restore to each individual the power to speak up for their own feelings and wishes. The aim of such a system of 'house meetings' will be partly to enable such issues to be addressed and resolved, and partly to create a climate of open and less defended communication so that conflicts and tensions can hopefully be handled productively at other times as well. The overall aim will be to lower some of the anxiety about issues of power which can lead to panicky reactions and sometimes to aggressive conflicts.

This sort of system is not always easy to establish or maintain (Ward 1995), but once established it can become central to the whole enterprise.

**Example 6.1 Establishing community meetings**

In a hostel supporting older adolescents with enduring mental health difficulties, the House

Meeting began as a regular informal talk around the supper table on a Monday night, when most of the residents had no other commitments. The residents themselves decided that they wanted to establish the group as a more formal meeting, because they felt that otherwise any discussions or decisions were less likely to be followed through by the staff or respected by the whole house. At first each of the residents took it in turn to chair the weekly meetings, but they soon decided that it was better for one person to hold the chair for a few weeks before handing it over, again in the belief that consistency would lead to greater confidence and thus better meetings.

As the meetings gained momentum, more staff began to make the effort to attend, and the status of the meetings developed further as the residents gained the confidence to express their views more directly to others, occasionally inviting local social workers or other support workers to join them. The meeting was clearly contributing to the residents' growing self-belief, and it gave them valuable lessons for life in the experience of discovering and asserting their own collective and individual power.

Another crucial factor in the above example was the encouragement and confidence in the residents shown by the manager, who consistently supported their attempts to formalise their meeting and to 'feel their way' into the experience of power. This ability to encourage others to realise their own power also requires confidence and a sense of personal security on the part of the leader and others, because otherwise they can very easily feel threatened by the young people's assertiveness and to react defensively, sometimes belittling or ignoring their efforts.

I have occasionally visited a home in which a system of 'House Meetings' or something similar has been tried but has failed to become established, and the critical factor here has often been the lack of a full and ongoing commitment to the system by the senior staff, and especially by the manager. 'Lip-service' or a half-hearted tolerance of such an approach on the part of senior staff will never be enough, and of course young people are finely attuned to any reluctance on the part of leadership to really share their power.

**The abuse of power**

This discussion of the dynamics of power in leadership would be incomplete without some acknowledgement that it is not uncommon for leaders to handle their own power badly. In all work-settings we will sometimes come across leaders who may bully and harass their staff, as well as instances of other staff treating each other in such ways, and sadly residential care homes are not exempt from this sort of behaviour.

One way of looking at bullying is to see it as a symptom of ineffective or absent leadership: bullies are very often trying to control or subordinate others over whom they either don't have legitimate authority, or over whom they *feel* they don't have enough control. In other words it may (perhaps paradoxically) be a sign of a weak or unconfident leader that they feel they need to resort to unfair coercion or worse in order to feel in control. This is no excuse for such behaviour of course, but this element may offer a clue as to how the problem needs to be addressed. Every organisation should have clear and value-led systems for the supervision of each person's work - including the work of leaders and managers - and if a leader is tending to bully or harass staff, then this is probably also an indication that their own work is not being effectively supervised. Supervision is certainly the arena in which the issue needs to be addressed, and those responsible for overseeing the work will need to be alert to the possibility of the misuse of power by leadership.

Bullying is rarely just a one-off incident: it tends to be self-perpetuating, and within a pattern of workplace intimidation a bullying leader will often make implicit threats about the future prospects of their victim. This sort of pattern is likely to carry on until it is confronted, although it can feel increasingly difficult for anyone to challenge. One of the reasons why it may be difficult to for others to challenge a bullying leader is that such behaviour doesn't always operate in the open or through direct means, but sometimes involves the bully drawing the victim into a closed world of fearful compliance in which the leader insists on the victim's acquiescence.

**Example 6.2 Sarah the bullied assistant**

Sarah was employed as a senior administrative assistant in a residential home. She was known to colleagues as a quiet, sensitive and efficient worker, and she was well-liked. Some months after a new manager was appointed to the home, Sarah began to feel that he was making excessive demands on her workload and being highly critical - often in quite personal terms - when she was unable to deliver work on time. He would always wait until there was nobody else in the office before making these verbal attacks on her and would sometimes then shut the office door and raise his voice until he was shouting at her.

Sarah felt increasingly upset and stressed by this behaviour and began to dread coming in to work, but as she had always been such a conscientious worker she felt ashamed of this fear and was reluctant to admit to anyone else that there was a problem. Eventually another colleague who had overheard the shouting asked Sarah what was going on, and advised her to speak to a senior manager at head office. Although Sarah was initially very anxious about taking such a step, with the support of a trade union colleague she did so, and this eventually led towards a resolution of the problem.

In this case the bullying was usually carried out away from other staff, which made it much harder for Sarah to confront, especially as this manager appeared to be much less controlling of other staff, leaving Sarah feeling that it must be somehow her own fault that she was being bullied. This self-blame on the part of the victim is another common aspect of bullying. It may also not be coincidental that in this case there appeared to be an element of sexism in the behaviour of the male manager's treatment of a female worker.

**Prejudice**

Prejudice involves making assumptions about others based on stereotyped and often negative views which usually stem from anxiety about difference - such as the assumptions that white people may have about black people as a group, that men may have about women, adults about children, and thus about any individual as somehow 'typical' of that group.

To illustrate how the dynamics of difference may weave in and out of leadership scenarios, we will focus here mainly on questions of gender, although parallel issues will arise in each of the other areas mentioned above, and often more powerfully when more than one issue is involved.

### *Gender*

Issues of gender are woven through the fabric of residential child care, particularly in the relationships between the young people, the staff and the manager. This is partly because of the broader themes of gender inequality throughout society, but partly also because many of the young people are likely to have had especially negative experiences of either male or female adults (or both), perhaps through experience with their parents but maybe also through encounters with teachers, police, foster carers and other professionals.

In particular, the young people may carry especially strong feelings about both mother- and father-figures which will influence how they relate with those occupying these roles. Residential care workers will be familiar with the unavoidable pitfalls of being seen as a parental figure. Some try to avoid these pitfalls by denying the parental element in their role, although there will always remain the basic fact that they are employed as responsible adults to help and support the young people and that this will inevitably lead to their sometimes being seen as 'parental'.

One extreme representation that I encountered of the way children in residential care may feel about parental figures - and mothers in particular - took place when I arrived at work one Sunday morning:

**Example 6.3 Mothers' Day**

As I walked down the drive from the main road I saw an effigy hanging from a tree in the front garden of the home. This had apparently been placed there by a group of young children from the home and it carried a slogan which read "Hang a mother for Mothers' Day". This graphic image, and the activity which had led to it, expressed the full rage and vindictiveness which some of the children felt towards the mother who they felt had let them down or metaphorically killed them off. It was a situation that needed careful handling if children's (and any visiting parents') feelings were to be respected: readers might find it useful to consider how they would handle this situation if they had to manage it.

At the same time it is not uncommon for children to also hold on to an idealised image of the perfect mother or father they wish they had had, or which they still want to believe they do have - and indeed for them to sometimes express both the idealisation and the denigration at the same time or to swing unpredictably between them. The strength of such ambivalence, and the confusion which it causes for young people, often contribute to the very mixed feelings which they bring to their relationships with staff and especially with the manager, who may be perceived as being in a highly-charged parental role.

Bearing this in mind, a female manager in a children's home may represent either a demon or a saviour to the young people, and often both at the same time. Children's wishes for rescue from their inner turmoil may be projected onto a 'maternal' manager, whom they may tend to see as either an idealised or a loathed figure - and she will of course have to be very careful in how she responds to such projections. This will not necessarily happen at a conscious level (such as when a young person may actually say 'You're as bad as my Mum') - it is just as likely to be acted out more indirectly and implicitly. So the leader may only really discover how she is seen as she finds herself struggling to cope with the heightened levels of anger or hostility she may be experiencing. At such moments, for instance, she may notice defensive feelings of her own being sparked off if she feels under personal attack, or she may realise that she has been drawn into collusive closeness by a young person who perhaps wants to see her as an idealised maternal figure.

One natural response to such pressures may be for the leader to try to respond with warmth and acceptance and to offer nurturing - though this may not work either. She cannot in reality, of course, be the universal or stereotypical mother to everyone, even though at some level she might wish she could be, but neither should she collude with the feeling that she is some kind of monster who is personally depriving children of their family life, which she may also be made to feel at times. She has to manage the differing expectations which the children (and sometimes their parents) may have of her and will probably aim to respond in a broadly consistent way to them all, and yet somehow still remain herself and true to herself.

Meanwhile a male leader may be subjected to the equivalent projections of being viewed as if in some way destructive, whether this means being seen as just as abusive or neglectful, or just as hostile or absent, as the children may have viewed their own father-figures as being. On the other hand, because of stereotyped views of male authority, occasionally the young people may treat a male manager with great caution and apparent respect - sometimes irritating the other staff by paying much more heed to the manager's word than to anyone else's. The manager has to guard against the self-delusion which such a pattern may produce, and accept that it may simply be a function of the role they are playing, or even of the fear which the young people feel for all male adults or male authority figures. Some young people may find relationships with their everyday care staff easier, but keep a special kind of resentment and rejection for the leader.

Clearly the above discussion also raises important questions about the broad stereotypes in society about male and female roles, about supposed masculine and feminine characteristics, and about the maternal and paternal aspects of parenting. I certainly don't want to suggest that a female leader will *only* experience difficulties in relation to supposedly 'feminine' or 'maternal' functions (or *vice versa* for male leaders). I do feel it is helpful, however, to acknowledge that - because of the young people's experience of what may sometimes have been extreme or distorted versions of parental roles - they may bring powerful and complicated assumptions to their interactions with leaders, based on these previous experiences. If leaders and teams can make regular opportunities in team meetings to discuss such dynamics and their respective experience of them, and if they can also extend such discussions to include the young people in them, then this opening-up of communication may help to reduce the 'acting-out' of the strong feelings which may exist in this area.

Of course young people will have their own strong feelings about other aspects of their own and other people's gender and these feelings will be still be at a formative and often changeable stage, leading at times to pain and confusion. Gender (like both ethnicity and racism) is an under-explored theme in residential child care and one that would repay much further attention.

## Sexuality in teams

Leaders are often at the centre of a set of powerful and often unspoken feelings in which everyone notices things about the leader, including not only their personal and emotional style, but also their 'presence', in terms of their levels of engagement, their interpersonal skills and the boundaries which they manage. Again it is the power element which infects the relationships and which, if not thought about and communicated about, can distort both perception and reality.

There is often also a covert element of sexuality in the relationship: the power of leadership may be experienced by some as a sexual challenge or even invitation, while the wish to influence or please the boss (or perhaps to fight the boss) may have this component too. People in organisational power may also exert a certain personal power and this may at times be experienced, or perhaps be used, in sexual terms; and in some cases there may be tensions between people's sexuality and their power. Words such as 'dominant' or 'submissive' to describe leaders and others give some of the flavour of these dynamics. An attractive and powerful leader who can invite individual loyalty may almost seduce people into compliance, although not necessarily consciously so.

In residential settings, people work closely together in emotionally charged situations, and often have to rely on each other for support and comfort when things become tense or confrontational. Given that all workplace relationships can develop a sexual component it is not surprising that this may also happen in the residential setting. Staff are often young and may be single or unattached: the demands and unsocial hours may make this a job that is difficult for those with their own family responsibilities to sustain. The staff may also be subject to frequent sexualised responses, comments or intrusive questions from the young people, and will often have to deal with extreme sexual acting-out among the young people. Such comments can all contribute to an atmosphere of heightened awareness of sexuality, which if not addressed explicitly may get acted out, even by those in the leadership role.

Relationships between staff members have special resonance in this setting because the young people, for all their difficulties, are likely to be adept at tuning in to the quality and nature of staff relationships, and sometimes to provoke, interfere, or at least comment, which may complicate things further. Additionally, because the young people may themselves have powerful and complicated feelings about their own sexuality, sometimes exacerbated by earlier abusive experiences, there may be a tendency for these feelings to find their way into the staff team, sometimes through indirect and unconscious means.

This all impinges on leadership, because the leader may get involved in trying to mediate - or worse, the leader may get drawn into such relationships or may even seek to get involved in them. This aspect of leader/team relationships may be the last to be acknowledged and discussed openly, and yet it may often turn out to underpin some of the difficulties that have to be dealt with. It is also the factor which can turn a difficult situation into an impossible one: impossible because any unacknowledged sexual dynamics in teams can become increasingly hard to 'name', especially in relation to the dynamics around the leader. In order for such issues to be safely discussed and resolved, it is again often invaluable to have an external team supervisor in a consultative role whose main aim will be to facilitate open and safe communication.

**From dependency to autonomy**

Because leaders are in a position of power and authority, others are to some extent dependent on them, firstly in a practical sense. People rely on their leaders for advice and guidance not only in relation to decision-making and policy, but also, as we have seen, for a sense of shared and even inspiring 'vision' which will help them to work together towards a common goal. However, the relationships between staff and leaders may evoke another kind of dependency, a feeling of being able to rely on someone for emotional support through difficult times, and a sense that the leader is resilient and tolerant enough to remain responsive despite being put to the test. As we saw in the earlier discussion about the unconscious elements in leadership, this dependency may also be experienced via the templates which we may all unwittingly bring with us - often based on much earlier experiences with parental and other key figures. Some workers may perceive their leader as stern and controlling, or distant and unavailable, sometimes without being aware of how their *own* unconscious templates may be affecting these perceptions and expectations around dependency.

Such expectations, which are often unspoken, may evoke a defensive reaction in some leaders, who in their enthusiasm to encourage independence and autonomy among their staff, may go too far in keeping them at arm's length and so may become emotionally distant from their team. On the other hand some leaders seem to relish this dynamic of dependency and have a 'need to be needed' which complicates the relationship unhelpfully, as we will see in the next chapter. This may show in their responses to the demands either from staff or especially from the young people, who are likely to have considerable unmet dependency needs of their own, as they may have been let down and treated badly by important adults throughout their lives.

Perhaps the key responsibility of the leader in this respect is to be aware of the dynamics around dependency with each individual and group and to offer thoughtful responses as appropriate. In most cases this will mean accepting a degree of dependency while also encouraging people to move towards a mature sense of their own relative independence and autonomy. People need to be able to make their own decisions at ground level without having to constantly 'refer up' for advice or instruction: this is partly a question of staff establishing their own level of authority. If child care workers are frequently having to respond to requests or demands from young people by saying "I don't know, I'll have to ask/check" they are unlikely to establish good working relationships with them, as the young people will soon learn to bypass or subvert staff whom they perceive as lacking authority or autonomy.

As in other areas, the leader therefore needs to strike a balance in managing the dependency needs of staff and young people, acknowledging their needs and responding appropriately to them but without getting drawn into inappropriate reactions. Once again this is an area in which leaders will especially benefit from having regular supervision and consultancy to ensure that they monitor themselves effectively.

**Summary**

From a starting point of drawing attention to the framework of values that underpins all care work including the leadership of such work, we have looked at the specific areas or power, prejudice and dependency. We have seen how such dynamics may affect the work at both conscious and unconscious levels and how it can be essential to gain the additional perspective of an external team and leadership consultant to address the more complicated dynamics of relationships and power within the caring team.

CHAPTER SEVEN

# The Leader as a Person

The focus of this book has been on the many personal and professional challenges facing leaders in residential child care settings, especially in terms of the interpersonal dynamics between leaders, their teams and the group as a whole. The real challenge for any leader is to be oneself and be true to oneself while also meeting the wide range of expectations and achieving the task expected of a leader. In this chapter we will focus on what this challenge means for leaders, and how they can remain human despite the demands of the job.

## The risk of isolation

We saw earlier that the leader can be seen as standing at a critical point in the organisation, at the fulcrum balancing its outer and inner worlds, or to put it another way, on the boundary between all the various groups and groupings involved. Either way, this is potentially an isolated position, and some leaders are tempted to deny or avoid this isolation by blurring the boundaries, getting too closely identified either with the outside world of senior management or with the inside world of the staff of the unit - or sometimes with the young people themselves, as we have also seen. None of these courses of action is helpful if taken too far, because in the long run the leader is equally accountable in all directions and may have to 'hold the line'. This is why it was proposed earlier that the true 'place' of leadership is *on* or close to the boundary. The personal price to be paid for holding this position is that the leader risks becoming too separate from others and therefore less effective, and that in the process he or she may experience anxiety in the form of loneliness or professional isolation.

### Example 7.1 Celia holds back

Celia was the manager of a long-established children's home run by a local authority. She was informed by senior management one day that within six months' time there was a plan to redesignate the home with a new and very different purpose, which would have major implications for the existing staff and children. She was asked not to disclose these plans until a firm decision had been made, to avoid unnecessary extra distress and uncertainty, and she agreed to this request even though it left her feeling disloyal both to her staff and to the children who might find that they had to move to new accommodation at short notice. She felt concerned for their future and guilty at holding knowledge that might affect them deeply and yet being unable to inform them. She was also aware that there was a risk that she might inadvertently convey something of the uncertain future which she knew the unit now had, perhaps by giving vague or ambiguous answers to innocent questions.

However, within a few weeks the plans had changed again because of an unrelated financial difficulty in the authority, and the proposal was shelved for a further twelve months. Celia was relieved and glad that she had not 'spilled the beans' in any way, but still felt uncomfortable in having to hold on to this knowledge and not being able to it with her staff. She now discussed these feelings again with her supervisor and began to negotiate a suitable way to discuss the plans with her senior staff, as a way of not only informing others but also consulting them on the range of future possibilities.

It is very common for leaders to have to confidentially hold on to important information, coming either from 'upstream' in the wider organisation or 'downstream' from individual staff members. In addition they often have to balance competing or conflicting views and emotions arising from different parts of the system, and have to decide not only where they stand in relation to these views, but also how to manage their own position strategically with regard to all parties. It has been an underlying theme of this book that leaders need to be wary of retreating into either denial of anxiety or a too-rigid adherence to formal procedure when faced with difficult decisions.

As we have seen, sometimes leaders get drawn into a position too far from the boundary - either too far inside or too far outside. Either way the risks to the organisation, and sometimes to the well-being of the leader, are considerable.

**Example 7.2 Jeff the withdrawing leader**

Jeff was the leader of a successful therapeutic unit for adolescents which had been running for many years. He had credibility with most of the staff and young people, although some of the senior staff began to feel too closely monitored by Jeff, who rarely left the building - and who in fact lived in a

> house adjoining the site. On the one hand, Jeff was always present, in every meeting of both staff and young people, and always contributed actively and even passionately. On the other hand, he would rarely venture out into the rest of the professional network with which the unit needed to relate, saying that he preferred to delegate that role to his deputy - although in reality he was avoiding these external contacts. He gradually became more and more suspicious of the outside network, feeling that many of these people did not really value or understand the nature of the work in the unit, and he often ended up in conflict with them, which would seem to be exactly what he had feared.
>
> As time went on, Jeff became increasingly isolated and so did the unit, because fewer social workers wished to make referrals to a place which had retreated so much from the rest of the world, and which had begun to develop a reputation for being 'difficult'. Meanwhile Jeff felt that this situation proved his point that the rest of the world was hostile and suspicious.

In the above scenario Jeff was unable to recognise that he was virtually painting himself and the unit into a corner, and his own isolation (which seemed to stem from his anxiety about working with other agencies) soon became 'enacted' in the whole unit, which would have risked closure through lack of business if the situation had continued for much longer. In this case the organisation called in a staff consultant to work intensively with Jeff towards re-positioning his role in the organisation, and things gradually began to change. This was a constructive solution to the problem: Jeff's line manager in the organisation was basically sympathetic to him, though increasingly frustrated, and could see the urgent need for the re-positioning. A less sympathetic line manager might have made life much harder for Jeff and for the unit - which shows again that good leadership within the unit does also depend on good leadership from outside it.

### Countering the risk of isolation

There are various ways in which the potential isolation of the role can be addressed, especially through the leader having regular access to supervision and mentoring, but also through their belonging to a peer support group and using external consultancy. It can be especially helpful to have more than one form of regular support, because the leadership role is so complex and includes so many different types of responsibility. For example, supervision within the line management structure of the organisation is essential in terms of keeping the unit broadly in line with its agreed task and properly co-ordinated with the overall task of the organisation. At the same time, however, it is also vitally important that the leader has reliable and regular access to *external* consultancy, in order to feel free to reflect openly and at times critically on the whole experience, including coping with the demands of head office, which may conflict with other hopes and expectations. Unfortunately, apart from in some therapeutic units, the valuable contribution of external consultancy is not often recognised, and it tends to be seen as an expensive luxury. However, it can certainly help a leader to avoid some of the pitfalls we have seen, such as becoming isolated or autocratic, or perhaps chronically indecisive due to anxiety.

Another element in the support system is likely to be the mutual support which leaders in similar units or organisations can offer each other if they can establish a supportive network in which they can perhaps hold regular meetings, as well as being available to each other for informal advice or solace at times of stress. One of the hazards of the growing privatisation of residential services in the UK has been that some leaders have begun to feel in competition with each other rather than being able to support each other, whereas in fact leaders have a responsibility not to get drawn into such rivalries, which rarely contribute to high quality services.

However, none of these forms of support will necessarily take away the reality that it can feel 'lonely at the top'. Perhaps what leaders need is what Winnicott called 'the capacity to be alone' and especially to be 'alone in the presence of others' (Winnicott, 1965) - which in this case means the ability to hold one's own position and authority without needing to seek escape or compromise. This involves the ability to know your own mind and not to allow it to be impinged upon by other people's anxieties, and to feel secure and resilient in the face of criticism or attack - but equally, to take proper account of others' concerns and not to retreat into an arrogant position of 'knowing it all'. The leader who can hold such a balanced role will have confidence in their own identity, knowledge and experience as well as the ability to communicate these to others for the benefit of the young people.

There is therefore a balance to be struck, because no leader is an island, and it is never helpful to place yourself in 'splendid isolation' as a leader, withdrawing from potential allies on all sides and issuing comments or orders from afar. A leader needs connectivity, i.e. links with all parties and especially with those in a position to share in leadership or to be consulted about making decisions or assessing situations.

**Example 7.3 Jan and her 'spot-checks'**

In one residential home which had gradually become quite dysfunctional, the leader, Jan (who lived half a mile down the road), had got into the habit of doing what she called 'spot checks' during

> her time off or when she was due to be elsewhere, by calling in unexpectedly to check up on the staff. This was highly disruptive and undermining to the team and especially to the deputy, who increasingly felt that she was not trusted. Taken overall, this pattern suggested an insecure and authoritarian leader who was unable either to lead effectively when she was present or to delegate sufficiently to allow the deputy to develop her own authority. There was also a blurring of roles in that the leader was virtually taking on the additional and quite inappropriate role of an 'unannounced inspector'.

In this case the leader was not only isolated but also somewhat paranoid - and she was certainly creating paranoid feelings in her staff. However, she had been able to sustain this position for some time through the combination of intimidating the staff and nevertheless impressing her Head Office because they thought she was running a 'tight ship', a perception that was finally overturned one day when an unannounced inspection by the real Inspection Unit was rudely interrupted by one of the boss's own flying visits!

**The leadership team**

The above example confirms that it is not always helpful to think of 'the leader' as an entirely separate individual. As we saw in Chapter One, he or she needs to build a leadership team which can work collaboratively on most of the issues and challenges that need to be faced. This team will include the deputy and perhaps intermediate team leaders, depending on the size of the organisation. The relationships within this 'core' of each home are of critical importance, as they will influence the whole system or network of relationships, and the best way to work on developing the leadership team is through regular and frequent meetings. The metaphor of the 'round table' approach to leadership seems especially fitting here, and this can even be emphasized by meeting around an actual round table. There also needs to be a continuity through time, of leadership 'going-on-being' even when senior managers are not physically present - in other words the spirit and overall agreed approach of the leadership team needs to be carried forward from one shift or day's (and week's) work to the next, regardless of which member of that team is on duty.

By contrast with the above example of Jan and her flying visits, this leadership team will need to evolve a culture of mutual trust and respect, and it is on this trust that delegation will be built. Delegation, of course, should not consist of the leader parcelling out the harder or more uncomfortable aspects of the leadership role and 'landing' other people with them. It works best when it fosters people's individual and collective talents, and when it enables the more anxiety-ridden tasks to be shared and managed jointly.

We saw in Chapter One the example of a residential home and school where the senior management team met every morning after the children went into school to review and plan, to co-ordinate the coming day's work and to anticipate factors which may need to be taken into account. This 'management' element in the meetings (reviewing, planning, co-ordinating) was also complemented by an explicit 'leadership' element, in which the leader of each unit would reflect on the issues facing them in their leadership role, which, in turn, sometimes allowed for further reflective discussion on aspects of leadership itself.

Smaller units may not have the resources or need for a full management team but at least it will be possible for the head and deputy or other senior person to meet every day with a similar brief. It may sometimes be argued that 'we are too busy to have that sort of daily meeting' - to which the obvious reply is that if the meeting were to become established as a forum for shared leadership and reflection, the general level of 'busyness' might be reduced because less time would need to be spent in reacting to unanticipated events.

Careful thought will need to go into deciding who should and should not be included in the leadership team. In one multi-unit campus that I visited the management team meetings included not only the head of each unit but also the head of the maintenance staff. However, team leaders began to feel that if they were to properly respect the principle of confidentiality it was not possible to report in these meetings as fully as they needed to on the issues arising with the young people in their units, as the head of maintenance was not otherwise party to any confidential information about the young people's family backgrounds. It was eventually recognised that this person's attendance at the meeting might be impeding one vital task of the meeting, which was to enable the team leaders to report and reflect on some of the matters currently arising in their units. However I am also aware of other places where there a different view is taken of relatedness, with 'support services' being more fully integrated into management at other levels.

## Confidence

In the earlier scenario of Jan and her 'spot checks' (Example 7.3), what seemed to underlie this leader's seemingly arrogant behaviour was a serious lack of confidence - not only her confidence in herself but also her confidence in others, and the theme of confidence has recurred throughout this book.

Confidence is an elusive and ambiguous quality: there are some people who appear to have more of it than is perhaps good for them, while some others seem to have less than they are entitled to. It is not just a question of believing in your own abilities but also of encouraging others to believe in you, and yet on the other hand avoiding getting caught up in your own myths. Some leaders inspire confidence: in other words, they inspire other people to feel confident in them and to feel more confident themselves. Others, meanwhile, have quite the opposite effect, so that people actually feel *less* confident when with them, perhaps because the leader seems too anxious or preoccupied to notice others' needs and therefore unable to contain their anxiety when necessary.

**Managing the 'burden' of leadership**

Because of the demands of the role and the emotional strain involved, it is also important that leaders manage their own personal resources and keep clear boundaries between their professional and their personal lives. It is no coincidence that some of the examples given in this book of where leadership has gone wrong have included an element of the blurring of these boundaries. This is no surprise: residential child care is often felt as a true vocation, in which people feel personally moved and motivated to put huge amounts of time and energy into supporting troubled children. But the reality is that this can easily turn into a burden or become over-preoccupying, and in fact leaders in particular will only be able to sustain their input if they also remain in control of their own personal boundaries.

Leaders therefore also need the self-discipline to know their own limits, to draw a line around their commitment, and monitor their input carefully. I have written elsewhere (Ward 2006) of the importance of finishing each day's work clearly and making the effort not to take home too much emotional 'baggage' - this may mean de-briefing in a handover meeting, writing up appropriate records before leaving, passing on important communications, and leaving as few loose ends as possible. Similarly at the end of a week or before going on leave, it is in everyone's interest that the leader makes sure everything is left clear and well recorded and communicated. These may seem very basic points, but they are worth repeating because without such attention to the fullest detail of communication, things often go wrong either for the unit or for the leader - who may otherwise carry on puzzling over uncompleted tasks or worrying about unresolved situations and those who must deal with them in the leader's absence.

### Positivity and life beyond the workplace

Beyond these perhaps rather defensive remarks about maintaining your boundaries, however, there is something else to be said about the 'Leader as a person'. Leaders are likely to be most effective when they can feel positive and creative, not only in their work but also in their own lives outside of work. For this reason, it is especially important for leaders to relax well, and to find and develop interests and activities work that will refresh and revive them and enable them to achieve a good balance in their life. There are many business-oriented texts which develop this theme, but not so many in the welfare field. One which I have personally found useful in this respect is '*Poetry and the Preservation of the Soul at Work*' by David Whyte (1994). Whyte was a corporate worker in the United States who learned after a period of intense stress how to handle work-related stress, and then found more meaning and balance in his life by developing his interest in poetry. Of course, for other people the interest which will achieve the same results may be anything from computer games to sky-diving: for some people it will be important to get as far away as possible from any connections with work, whereas for others their outside interests may not be so far removed but at least they are separate from work and from what Buddhists call the 'ten thousand things' which crowd in on us in everyday life (and especially in work life). Yet others will find that it is their faith that is the unifying and consoling factor that helps them to manage and contain the competing pressures of work and home life.

One function of such outside interests may be to enable people to develop different areas of strength and confidence, other personal networks of friendship and activity and to therefore feel more 'whole' and rounded as an individual, which will in turn have a positive impact back in the world of work.

**The need to be needed**

One personality trait which is actively *un*helpful in leaders is an excessive need to be liked or needed. The need to be liked can push you into always 'agreeing with the last speaker', or not feeling able to challenge others with whom you disagree, or perhaps being too lenient in following through decisions which may be unpopular though necessary. The need to be needed is perhaps different: it may become apparent in leaders if they encourage excessive dependency in team members, perhaps by not delegating enough, or by imposing inappropriate 'cut-off points' in people's levels of decision-making or responsibility, and thus retaining more power for themselves. On the other hand we should bear in mind that there may be developmental issues here. We talked in Chapter One about leadership as an unfolding process, and it is not uncommon that a new leader may start out by holding a lot of power and decision-making very centrally, but with a view towards delegating as part of an ongoing developmental process. In this way, delegation can involve showing increasing trust in people to carry out tasks which the leader knows about from the inside rather than simply trying to reduce his or her own workload. As leaders grow into the role, and as the team members and the leader accommodate to each other, the relationship will evolve into one in which all parties can rely on each other and trust each other, rather than any individual needing to be needed.

**Summary**

We have now come full circle. I began this book on a very personal note, and told the story of my own shaky beginnings as a leader, which eventually led me into finding proper confidence and developing more effective authority. Others will have made their own journeys in this role, though not all may have been as dramatic as mine. I would certainly hope that others will take on the role with more experience and well-founded confidence than I had, as well as with the full range of support systems which are so necessary.

So now we are reaching the conclusion of this study of leadership and again we have found ourselves returning to a personal theme, this time looking at the leader as a person and how they need to manage their own emotional economy as well as that of the unit itself. We have seen that on the one hand leaders need to remain both thoroughly engaged in their work and involved with staff and young people, without at the same time having an excessive need to be either liked or needed. They need to be personal, committed and relational without pushing the boundaries of charisma or 'transformational leadership' into attention-seeking or even bullying. They need to have a clear set of values and the ability to model those values in action in their dealings with people at all levels. And finally they need to work with not only the conscious, rational complexities of the task, but also with the unconscious and irrational elements which it includes. As I said in the introduction, leadership is a tall order and a demanding role, though it is also one which is deeply worthwhile. There remains one last area to consider in the final chapter.

CONCLUSION

# What makes leadership work?

As this journey comes to an end I want to shift the emphasis one more time. The book has focused on the roles and tasks of leadership, and especially on the relationship-based work which needs to go on at all levels, sometimes formally and sometimes informally. In emphasizing the relational dynamics of the work, however, I do not want to deny the organisational structure within which any children's home or other residential establishment is set. Even the most skilled and insightful leader will struggle and may fail if the organisational constraints within which he or she is trying to operate are unhelpful or undermining. Just as we saw in

Chapter 2 in the analogy of the football manager who triumphs with one team but fails with another - sometimes it can be the Chair of the Board who actually loses the match without setting foot on the pitch - so sometimes it may be the organisation which fails the leader.

There therefore remains one important question: 'What makes leadership work?' In other words, what conditions and resources will provide the best opportunities for high quality leadership to flourish in residential care and how can other systems support and contribute to this? These closing remarks are addressed primarily to those with overall or external responsibility for overseeing residential services, as well as to those in the leadership role who may sometimes wonder why life has to have so many uphill scrambles. I will suggest four main external conditions or contributing factors to successful leadership in residential services.

**First**, the larger organisation within which the residential home is situated has to be clear and direct about the precise task expected of the home. This is a matter not just of setting broad remits such as 'short-stay' or 'preparation for fostering', but of being as clear as possible about the particular profile of young person for whom the home is intended, including in particular the level and intensity of their emotional need. There also needs to be clarity and agreement about the expected length of stay and the 'hoped-for outcome' for each child, as well as about the nature of the work to be undertaken. Such areas need to be on the one hand clear and well-defined but also subject to ongoing review with the leader / manager of the home.

**Second**, within this structure there needs to be clarity about the range and scope of the leader's authority; in particular the leader needs to hold key responsibility for decisions about all admissions and departures of young people and all comings and goings of staff. In many organisations some of these decisions will be taken at 'panel' or committee meetings, or in the equivalent management meetings in private organisations, but if the leader is going to be able to work with full authority and 'ownership' of the task, it will be essential that he or she retains a critical role within such decisions. A disempowered leader is no leader at all.

**Third** there needs to be a range of expert support services provided for the leader in terms of both line management and external consultancy. We have seen throughout this book that it is only with clear lines of accountability that the leader can have true authority and appropriate confidence. In addition, and regrettably still something of a rarity, is the importance of the leader having regular access to external consultancy or mentoring. A relatively small ongoing investment of resources in such an external support system will pay for itself many times over.

**Fourth** and most importantly is the 'bottom line': the home and its leadership need to be adequately resourced to fulfil their task, with proper funding for all aspects of staffing including the essential elements of support, supervision, training and development. It will be within the manager's remit to make the best and most effective use of resources but it is the overall responsibility of the employing organisation to ensure that they are in place.

None of these conditions will guarantee effective leadership of course, but without them even the most able leader may struggle.

# Acknowledgements

I am very grateful to Jonathan Stanley for the original commission to write a paper on leadership, which came at a time when I was out of action and needed reminding that I might still have something to offer; also to Stuart Hannah for picking up that paper and using it in his teaching, which convinced me that it was worth turning it into hard copy for this edition. Many other people have offered encouragement and support, sometimes perhaps without knowing it, during my work on this manuscript, including Laura Steckley, Roger Hennessey, Juliet Miller, Deborah Best, Linnet McMahon, Jenny Cunningham, Thom Garfat, Terry Philpot and Rich Rollinson. I would also like to thank those who supported and encouraged me in my own residential leadership role: Paddy Barry, Christine Bradley and Caroline Whitehead, as well as the staff we appointed.

Special thanks are due to Thea Abbott who offered the chance of publication in this form and gave consistently helpful advice both on the content of the book and on the details of preparing it for publication. Without her help this book would certainly not have seen the light of day. Lastly and most of all, thanks to my dear wife Mary for her love and support in this and all our other projects.

# REFERENCES

Anglin, J. (2002) *Pain, Normality and the Struggle for Congruence: Reinterpreting Residential Care for Children and Youth.* New York, Haworth Press.

Bion, W. (1962) *Learning from Experience.* London, Heinemann.

Burton, J. (1997) *Handbook of Managing Residential Care.* London, Routledge.

Casement, P. (1990) *On Learning from the Patient.* London, Routledge.

Collie, A. (2002) Opportunistic Staff Development Strategies in Therapeutic Communities. *Therapeutic Communities* 23 (2) 125-132.

Collins, T. and Bruce, T. (1984) *Staff Support and Staff Training* London, Tavistock.

Danbury, H. and Wallbridge, D. (1989) Directive teaching and gut learning: The seminar technique and its use in video-based role-play learning. *Journal of Social Work Practice*, May, 53-67.

Ford, T., Vostanis, P., Meltzer, H., and Goodman, R. (2007) 'Psychiatric disorder among British children looked after by local authorities: comparison with children living in private households', *British Journal of Psychiatry*, **190**, pp. 319-325.

Fulcher, L. and Ainsworth, F. (2005) Group Care Practice with Children Revisited. Chapter 1 in : Fulcher, L. and Ainsworth, F. (ed) *Group Care Practice with Children and Young People Revisited.* New York, Haworth.

Hennessey, R. (2011) *Relationship Skills in Social Work.* London, Sage.

Hicks, L., Gibbs, I., Weatherly, H. and Byford, S. (2007) *Managing Children's Homes: Developing Effective Leadership in Small Organisations.* London, Jessica Kingsley.

Hinshelwood, R.D. (1990) *What happens in groups. Psychoanalysis, the individual and the community.* London, Free Association Books.

Howe, D. (2008) *The Emotionally Intelligent Social Worker.* Basingstoke, Palgrave Macmillan.

Huczynski, A. (1993) Explaining the succession of management fads. *The International Journal of Human Resource Management.* 4 (2) 443 - 463.

Jones, H.D. (1970) *Leadership in Residential Child Care* (Convocation Lecture, NCH). London, NCH.

Kendrick, A (ed.) (2007) *Residential Child Care: Prospects and Challenges (Research Highlights in Social Work Series)* London, Jessica Kingsley.

Lao Tsu, (1972) *Tao te Ching* USA Random House.

Miller, S. (2004) What's going on? Parallel process and reflective practice in teaching. *Reflective Practice* 5 (3) 383-393.

Milligan, I. & Stevens, I., (2006) *Residential Child Care: Collaborative Practice* London, Sage.

Obholzer, A and Roberts, V.Z. (eds) (1994) *The Unconscious at Work. Individual and Organizational Stress in the Human Services.* London, Routledge.

Rollinson, R. (2003) What a long strange trip it's been. In: Ward, A., Kasinski, K., Pooley, J. and Worthington, A. (ed.) *Therapeutic Communities for Children and Young People.* London, Jessica Kingsley.

Ruch, G.M., Turney, D. and Ward, A. (2010) *Relationship Based Social Work. Getting to the Heart of Practice.* London, Jessica Kingsley.

Shapiro, E.R. and Carr, W. (1991) *Lost in familiar places: creating new connections between the individual and society.* New Haven, London, Yale University Press.

Shohet, R (1999) Whose Feelings am I feeling? Using the concept of projective identification. In Hardwick, A. & Woodhead, J. (ed.) (1999) *Loving Hating and Survival. A Handbook for all who work with troubled children and young people.* Aldershot, Ashgate.

Sinclair, I. and Gibbs, I. (1998) *Children's homes: a study in diversity.* Chichester, Wiley.

Smith, M. (2009) *Rethinking Residential Child Care: Positive Perspectives*, Bristol, Policy Press.

Steckley, L. (2012) Touch, Physical Restraint and Therapeutic Containment in Residential Child Care. *British Journal of Social Work* 42 (3) 537-555.

Toynbee, P. (2014, May 13) Now troubled children are an investment opportunity. *The Guardian.*

Ward, A. (1995) Establishing community meetings in a children's home. *Groupwork*, 8 (1) 67-78.

Ward, A. (2002) Building a Team. in: Seden.J and Reynolds, J. (eds) *Social Care Management in Practice.* Buckingham, Open University Press.

Ward, A. (2004) Towards a theory of the everyday: the ordinary and the special in residential care. *Child and Youth Care Forum.*

Ward, A. (2006) *Working in Group Care. Social Work and Social Care in Residential and Day Care Settings. Second Edition.* Bristol, Policy Press.

Ward, A. (2014) 'Ah, but I was so much younger then ...' *Relational Child and Youth Care Practice*, 27 (2).

Whyte, D. (1994) *The Heart Aroused: Poetry and the Preservation of the Soul at Work.* New York, Random House.

Winnicott, D.W., (1965) The Theory of the Parent-Infant Relationship, in: *The Maturational Processes and the Facilitating Environment.* London, Hogarth Press and the Institute of Psychoanalysis.

# LIST OF PRACTICE EXAMPLES

# INDEX